Dynamiting the Siskiyou Pass

AND OTHER SHORT STORIES FROM OREGON AND BEYOND

Bill Meulemans

HELLGATE PRESS   ASHLAND, OREGON

DYNAMITING THE SISKIYOU PASS
And Other Stories from Oregon and Beyond
©2023 Bill Meulemans

Published by Hellgate Press

(An imprint of L&R Publishing, LLC)

Hellgate Press
72 Dewey St.
Ashland, OR 97520
email: *sales@hellgatepress.com*

Cover and Interior Design: L. Redding

ISBN: 978-1-954163-68-3

Printed and bound in the United States of America
First edition 10 9 8 7 6 5 4 3 2 1

Books by Bill Meulemans

*The Presidential Majority: Presidential Campaigning
in Congressional Elections* (1970)

Making Political Choices: An Introduction to Politics (1989)

Belfast: Both Sides Now (2013)

*How the Left and Right Think: The Roots of Division
in American Politics.* (2019)

*Dynamiting the Siskiyou Pass and Other Short Stories
from Oregon and Beyond* (2023)

Belfast Flashbacks (Publication Pending)

Contents

Foreword

I spent my first decade in Oregon tucked away in remote corners of Oregon's Rogue Valley, trying to shake my head clear of elite academic theories in order to learn enough survival skills to face the social and economic collapse that was, I was somehow sure, just around the corner. As the Nixon years gave way to the ten-minute Ford Administration and then the Carter years, an older yearning to get into the fray—I had Presidential ambitions around the same time I played Little League baseball—flared back up. I dropped back in.

The first step was part-time classes at Southern Oregon State College, now Southern Oregon University, in Ashland, fifteen miles up Interstate 5 from the California border. If you were on that campus in 1980 with even marginal interest in how politics works, Bill Meulemans was part of your life. I don't think a year's gone by since then that I haven't talked to an Oregonian who's named him as an important mentor.

There are a lot of reasons for that: the base of knowledge he brought to political science, paired with an active curiosity to learn more; a continuous willingness to question what he himself believed; the interest and energy he invested in every student that came to him; a knack for blending political theory and practice, especially when it came to how campaigns are won and lost. The teaching that stuck with and guided me when I entered elective politics was the tongue-in-cheek sorting of voters into "sinners" (those who would never in a million years vote for you), "saints" (those who are solidly with you, essentially your "base") and "savables" (the subset of voters, vanishingly rare these days, who aren't fully committed to either you or your opponent). Winning candidates spend a small percentage of their precious time and energy thanking and energizing the saints; everything else is directed towards the savables. Do not give in to the urge to pull the sinners over to your side (a potent urge for those of us whose collection of high school debate trophies left us thinking we're irresistibly persuasive). That's time wasted. Wasted time loses races.

That's just one of the gifts I've received from Bill over the years. Top of the list is an endearing friendship, even though we've shared little time together since he left SOU to do landmark work on political conflict in Ireland and elsewhere. Hearing his voice on the phone takes me back to conversations on gentle Ashland afternoons on his shady back porch, hearing his shrewd, human and deeply humane take on current politics—the individual and collective decisions we make on how we're going to live together. That practical and gentle perspective shines through the vivid stories of this book from first to last.

I found it an immense pleasure to read. Assuming that you're interested in what makes people tick, how that plays out in our politics, and how all of it can be nudged towards the kind of world we'd like to live in, I think you will, too.

Oregon State Senator Jeff Golden
Salem, Oregon
March 27, 2023

Preface

"Put down your pencils,
I'm going to tell you a story…"

When I said, "Put down your pencils," I found that my college students listened with a greater purpose. Their pencils were down, but their minds were more open than usual. They wanted to hear a story – to visualize the involvement of real people in a particular situation. I also discovered that they gained a greater understanding of a topic in which I was personally involved. Students, like everyone else, love to hear a personalized version of a tale. It makes everything come to life.

Stories let us share information in a way that creates a human connection. It catches our attention and engages us at a personal level. We are much more likely to understand an event if the background is highlighted. Knowing how it happened makes it come alive in our minds.

Is there any better way to learn than through a story? How else can we shine a bright light into all the dark corners of life? Hearing or reading an account of a new adventure is an exciting way to take a trip without leaving home. A well-told story is the next best thing to being there.

Don Hewitt, the producer of *60 Minutes*, the longest running prime-time program on American television repeatedly told his correspondents, "Tell me a story." It turns out that his call for a story is still the reason for the program's success. Every segment draws us into an important topic. It works on television and it works in real life. We all identify with dramatic stories. There's a special transformation when we imagine what we would do in a similar circumstance. There's no substitute for a good tale with a built-in lesson at the end.

This book is a personalized series of stories that highlight how life has evolved in Oregon and elsewhere since the 1960s. It is presented through the eyes of someone who treasured every minute of the unusual turn of events from then to now.

ONE

A Pleasant Caldron

There's a natural tendency to fall in love with Ashland, Oregon. It happened to me in two days. First, I drove through the downtown plaza that was so quaint and inviting. Then, almost by accident, I drove into the 100-acre Lithia Park as it wound up through a picturesque little valley with a bandshell and many places to just sit and contemplate life. Clearly, the Park was designed for nature lovers. On that first day I saw a deer grazing up on a hill. There were children throwing bread crumbs to the ducks in the ponds just behind the trees. To top off the scene, there was a creek that meandered through the Park down behind the plaza. What was not to love?

For me, coming to Ashland was like opening a series of Christmas presents. During my first two days in town, I opened a couple of presents each day as I explored the small-town setting with a touch of a sophistication that I had not seen before. Like so many other people who've had the same experience, I was ready to settle down and make it my home.

There were plenty of college teaching positions available when I got out of graduate school, but one caught my eye. I had heard about an opening at Southern Oregon College (now Southern Oregon University) in Ashland. It was an opportunity to teach political science in a liberal arts college in a small-town setting, nestled at the foot of the Siskiyou Mountains near the California border. It was love at first-site.

Ashland is an upscale, artsy, community known for the Oregon Shakespeare Festival and its charming atmosphere. The city has a progressive reputation that attracts people from all over the country. More than 100,000 people flock to Ashland every year to see world-class theatrical productions. The motto is "stay four days, see four plays." Southern Oregon University prides itself with a well-qualified faculty and a culturally-diverse student body. The pubs and book shops of Ashland are filled with actors and academicians. It's a great place to live.

But there is an "underground" dimension in this part of Oregon that is not noticed by outsiders. In reality Ashland is a liberal enclave surrounded by a region of Oregon that has been friendly to the Ku Klux Klan. In the 1920s Klan members wore their full regalia as they were photographed marching proudly past the city library down Siskiyou Boulevard in Ashland's 4th of July Parade. During these times there were stories about the Sheriff of Jackson County and several deputies being Klansmen. This part of Oregon had "sundown laws" that served as a warning to Black folks that they "shouldn't let the sun set on their backs" in the Rogue Valley.

But when I arrived in southern Oregon in 1964, most of the Klan hoods and robes had been put away in the hall closets, but the old attitudes lingered on with conservative activists and timber-products workers. There were still local folks who saw themselves as the defenders of a conservative, whites-only society that proudly upheld "American" values. There was also a strong dose of anti-Communism sentiments along with a gun culture that had a national reputation. Outside of town there was an unusual number of pickup trucks with gun racks in the back window. Some said affectionately this was a "little piece of Alabama tucked away in Oregon."

The hinterlands belonged to the hardhats, but there was an identifiable group inside of Ashland that was counter-culture. There was a patchwork of operating communes where young people shared their work and incomes in a very progressive environment. On a typical evening in Ashland, one had a choice of going to meetings on gay rights, home-made jewelry-making, or hearing about the finer points of Trotskyite theory. The mayor of Ashland was a self-proclaimed socialist and one candidate for the city council was a long-time sympathizer of the Communist Party. Ashland was a left-wing hub with right-wing spokes that spread out in every direction. People outside of the city were constantly shocked by the kinds of things that went on there.

Strangely, the situation was pretty much of a one-way street. The liberal elite inside of Ashland had little awareness or concern about those outside the city limits; they didn't know about them and didn't care. But right-wing folks in the outside areas knew exactly what was going on in Ashland. People in the surrounding cities of Medford, Central Point, Grants Pass, and Klamath Falls watched local TV and read the daily newspapers. Folks in other parts of Jackson, Josephine, and Klamath counties had real concerns about how much the progressive element inside of Ashland was changing the political/social culture of southern Oregon. There were candidates elected in Ashland that wouldn't have stood a chance outside the city limits. I had friends on both sides of the divide, and it was very clear that some right-wing folks in the Valley felt they were outsiders. They brought up the subject repeatedly. I was constantly amazed by the opposing orientations of the two groups. They lived in two different worlds.

Southern Oregon was a melting pot that never melted. There was no blending between the contending political/social clusters. Tourists could stroll the streets of Ashland enjoying the yuppie shops without realizing that there were right-wing and left-wing groups hiding in the hills nearby who saw themselves as revolutionaries. Few visitors to southern Oregon knew that this region was the home of opposing political underground movements. There were all sorts of clandestine operations going on that were not noticed by governmental officials.

I realized early on that there was an opportunity to bring leaders from both sides into my classroom. I began offering a course titled, "Political Extremism in America" in which I focused on comparing and contrasting ideological leaders of the left and right in local politics. In my course on "Oregon Politics," I also brought in elected officials from throughout the state. It was during the mid-1960s, a time of clashing ideologies in American politics. The pendulum was swinging back and forth from left to right in every corner of the country.

Upon my arrival in 1964, Barry Goldwater won the Republican presidential nomination with the support of many local right-wing voters, but he was trounced across the country. A few years later in 1972, a leading liberal, George McGovern, won the Democratic presidential nomination, but he was defeated by an even greater national margin. In the meantime, the Vietnam War was raging, the Black Panthers were on the streets in urban areas, and the Students for a Democratic Society were gearing up to shut down college campuses. Here in Oregon, there were right-wing militia groups in the mountains who had a cache of weapons (inside of caves) encased in a protective coating. Less than twenty miles away, in a hidden valley, there was a smaller, left-wing faction that dreamed of radicalizing the West Coast. Strangely, both sides knew of the other, but they were more interested in getting ready to fight than actually attacking each other.

Getting to know folks in the right-wing underground was a slow process for me. I spent lots of evenings going to events around the Valley to attend meetings that featured traveling "true-believers" full of conspiracy theories who warned of an impending Communist takeover that could bring the United States to its knees. Every few weeks there would be a speaker in Medford or Grants Pass who came in from the outside with the same message: "It's worse than you think and we've got to be ready to fight back." I got to know the local guys who sat in the front row at each meeting and didn't miss a word. It wasn't long before we were on a first-name basis. We actually became friends. They talked at length about their dedication to fighting Communists, but they felt it was a lonely task because most people in Rogue Valley were too busy raising their families and didn't really share the feeling of being on the front lines of an attempted Communist take-over.

Most Oregonians got their news about militant groups by reading the newspapers or watching TV specials. Yet in the Rogue Valley, all I had to do was just drive a few miles out of town where I could meet with folks that were on the cutting-edge of extremist movements. They were easy to miss because they seldom did anything that attracted attention. My strategy was to go to their meetings and ask the question, "Do you have any idea of why this is happening?" I was constantly amazed by what I heard. There were small segments dotted around the Valley that saw a very different political/cultural/religious reality.

One of my earliest contacts was with a religious sect that believed they were involved in an epic struggle involving the fate of our entire country. They showed me a picture of an FBI show-badge with the number "666" on it which they said was the "sign of the beast." Their leader told me that the badge was a sign from God that the Devil had taken over the US Department of Justice and probably all of Washington, D.C. He said, "Everything that happens there must be viewed through that perspective." In his view, this was a justification for revolution. It was a holy crusade that could not be lost.

The leader of that church was a preacher who carried a gun. He warned that Christians should take up arms and prepare for Armageddon. His group met in a run-down building they called "The Valley Miracle Center." There were stories of people whose eyesight had been restored and cripples who were able to walk. I attended meetings in which people were "speaking in tongues," but I never met anyone who had been healed. He and others in the church felt under-appreciated by the vast majority of Americans who weren't paying any attention to what they thought was a real demonic threat.

Most of these men were law-abiding folks in theory, but there were a few in the Rogue Valley that had already crossed the line. One leader from Grants Pass (who I didn't know) was arrested by federal agents for having a cache of stolen military small arms along and an anti-tank weapon he carried in the trunk of his motor-home. Another man in Central Point I knew well, was arrested in his home by Treasury Agents who found that he had a whole sheet of $20 bills on his kitchen table that had not been cut yet. His defense was that he was going to use the money to support his political efforts. Knowing of his disorganized personal demeanor,

I wasn't surprised to learn that the counterfeit bills were of poor quality.

One member of a southern Oregon right-wing group kept telling me, "Politics is about bullets, not ballots." That particular person was one I would call a "super-patriot." He said every time he read the Constitution it brought tears to his eyes. He and his comrades professed a great love of their country, and they were ready to fight another revolution out of fear that leftists were poised to take over the nation. They spent a lot of time planning for the future.

On the other side were left-wing groups that had migrated in from northern California. These were ardent environmentalists from Oakland and San Francisco who were planning to sabotage the timber-products industry. There were communes nestled into valleys that dead-ended in the high timber. The Siskiyou mountains along the California/Oregon border were a perfect hiding place for self-styled activists who were making preparations for a show-down they believed could come any day.

Most people in southern Oregon didn't know about the underground activists that were hiding out in plain sight. In some respects, the area was an ideal breeding ground for survivalists, super-patriots, hippies, and marijuana growers. An unsuspecting person didn't have to go too far off the beaten track to be in an area where they were not welcome. I knew of several remote areas that were off-limits to the outside world. Law enforcement officers knew about the nests of "gun nuts," and others, but the general orientation of the police was to leave well enough alone.

There was a strong tradition of rugged individualism in this part of Oregon. Many who came here wanted to be left alone. Both left- and right-wing groups were seeking an independence from the regular restrictions that applied to everyone else. Yet along with that sense of freedom came the feeling of being surrounded by unseen enemies that were closing in on them. The will to fight back was always present. There was a defensive characteristic among these lonely stalwarts at both ends of the political spectrum.

During the Cold War, several survivalist groups from around the country came to southern Oregon because it was far away from military bases and major cities that would be targets in the event of a nuclear war. They also reckoned that this part of Oregon would be safer because it was not down-wind from areas that would be contaminated by nuclear radiation. These folks made no attempt to integrate into the Rogue Valley. The only way I knew of their existence was because some of these new arrivals took my Political Extremism course. They told me they wanted to learn about extremist groups so they could defend themselves in the event there was a breakdown of society. They lived off the beaten path and just wanted to be left alone.

There's always been a strong isolationist, anti-government element in southern Oregon that dates back many years. Folks in the southern part of the state have regularly distrusted government at all levels. Many guests in my classes boasted that they didn't pay taxes of any kind. Others said that they had purposely ignored building codes and inspectors when building and remodeling buildings in remote areas. They boasted on the number of guns they had at home. Most of them were proud that tax levies in their communities faced tough opposition from local voters. Josephine Country had the lowest property tax in the state, yet they turned down a levy on police protection that forced the sheriff to lay off most of the deputies and release some local prisoners. Many folks in southern Oregon distrusted any kind of governmental activity.

Folks in these parts of rural Oregon have long felt alienated from the more densely populated areas near Portland, Salem, and Eugene. More than 40 percent of Oregon's population lives in the Portland metro area. Folks in eastern and southern Oregon feel like they are at the end of the pumpkin vine. There's been a move among several counties of southern Oregon to join with rural parts of northern California to form a new state called "Jefferson." Recently there's been a similar move with eleven counties of eastern Oregon voting to join the state of Idaho.

The voting patterns of rural and urban Oregon also differ widely. In 2020, for example, Democrat Joe Biden won the state with 56.9 percent of the vote, but he carried only 8 of Oregon's 36 counties. Donald Trump won the expansive rural areas, but Biden carried the cities by a comfortable margin. Typically, eastern and southern Oregon are solidly Republican while the urban areas of the northern part of the state are reliably Democratic. The Interstate 5 corridor passes through counties that include more than 80 percent of Oregon's population. There are many parts of the state that are seldom noticed by the city folks who hold a large majority.

The rural/urban split is a constant source of conflict. Often it is more important to find out what part of the state people are from than to find out if they are a Republican or a Democrat. To an outsider, Oregon seems to be one happy family, but there's a lot of disagreement boiling just below the surface.

TWO

Dynamiting the Siskiyou Pass

Interstate 5 is the main thoroughfare on the West Coast of the United States. The interstate freeway stretches all the way from Canada to the Mexican border. One of the most vulnerable points of the highway is the Siskiyou Pass located on the California/Oregon border. The Pass has an elevation of 4,310 feet where it cuts through the mountainous area. Keeping it open is of vital importance to interstate commerce and national defense. But in the mid-1960s there was a small group of self-appointed militia members who were prepared to dynamite the Siskiyou Pass.

It was a stunning surprise to me when I heard the plans of four men in Medford, Oregon, who had plans to dynamite the Pass in order to block an invasion of Communists they believed where going to sweep up through Oregon all the way to Seattle. I actually stumbled on the information while talking to several men that spoke about an armed invasion from California. At first their comments were rather vague, but all that changed one evening after four of them spoke in one of my classes at the college. By this time, they knew me pretty well and were inclined to let down their guard a bit and tell me certain things about their operations.

After my students left the classroom, these men told me that their main task was to get ready to dynamite the Siskiyou pass and block the Interstate 5 freeway from California in the event of an invasion from northern California. They said they had "intelligence" that there was a build-up of Communists in the forest lands on the California side of the summit, and that the enemy was forming an invading army that would use Interstate 5 to advance north and fan out in Portland and Seattle. I asked if they had seen the threatening army. They said no, but they were certain they were there. One of the guys thought that the invading army was mostly Chinese Communists, the other three said they were sure that they were "California Radicals" from the Bay Area. At any rate, these four men were getting ready to stop them at the pass.

A sense of duty prevailed with these four modern patriots. They wanted to be a part of something bigger than themselves – perhaps a part of history. One said he felt a little bit like a modern Paul Revere – warning this generation of Americans that they were being invaded. All of them kept the dynamite in the trunks of their cars so it would be ready to use when the time came.

I soon discovered that the plan to "close the pass" was not just idle chatter. They told me they had practiced several dry runs whereby their leader would call the other three on the phone during the night or early in the morning to see how quickly they could drive from their homes in Medford to the Siskiyou Summit. It was a twenty-six mile trip and they said their best time was thirty-seven minutes (on a stop-watch) to arrive and place their charges in dug out locations alongside the freeway. They were really proud of how fast they were able to put the charge in holes that had already been dug.

Later I drove up the freeway by myself to the summit but could not find any dug-out holes for the explosives. Actually, the highway through the pass at the Siskiyou Pass was quite wide and I did not see how they could close down the freeway. I don't know anything about dynamite, but they must have had a fair amount to blow up that pass. I asked them about the specific area where they would put the charge. They sensed my doubts on the operation and assured me they had stolen several boxes of high-grade dynamite from an abandoned mining operation, "more than enough to do the job."

This was their mission, and they saw themselves as "soldiers" who were ready to defend the whole Pacific Northwest against a possible invasion. I recall that they had an absolute devotion to the cause. They had an overwhelming sense of obligation to defend the rest of us who didn't know that an invasion was imminent. Their leader was a retired US Navy Seal who told me he was more than willing to give his life to "our country." He said that stopping the invasion would be the "most important thing in his life."

My relationship with these folks was always friendly. I discovered early on that they would be more likely to bare their souls if they thought I would give them a fair hearing. All I had to do was ask. One evening after a get-together in Medford, I pushed a bit beyond the conversation we had earlier. I asked why they carried guns on those trips up the mountain to put the dynamite in place? They looked at me with disbelief: "Why wouldn't we carry guns?" the leader asked. Then he went on to say, "What if someone tried to stop us?" I could tell that they knew the next question: "If government agents or the state patrol tried to stop you, what would you do?

The silence was awkward. They didn't want to answer at first. Then the leader said he felt the obligation to defend this country no matter what the authorities might do. To him the most important thing was stopping the invasion from the south. They all looked at each other with blank stares as they each nodded their heads. I didn't disagree. I followed up with the question of whether "the government had the right to overrule them," but I could tell they didn't want to go there.

After that exchange I thought a lot about self-appointed patriots of the right and left, and how the political system should react to those who were willing to use deadly force. The ones I knew viewed government as part of the problem. Being anti-Communist and anti-government in their minds were almost the same thing.

In their minds the concept of "America" was a symbol elevated above what most of us would see as the government. They had a higher calling: it was to defend the rest of us even if we opposed them. I didn't know how to respond to that idea because that put their group at a level beyond everyone else. They saw themselves as a truly patriotic, independent force.

In their minds the task of defending the country was more important because almost no one else was aware of the impending danger. It was assumed that the US military had been misled by shadowy figures that were controlled by our enemies. "You can't count on the police or the army," they said. Their assumption was that nearly everyone else had been "bought off" or were unaware of the situation. I asked "how many people in the Rogue Valley knew about this threat? They shook their heads with a resigned smile commenting that the great majority of the American people won't give much thought to losing their country until it's too late.

One of the characteristics shared by these revolutionaries was a sense of destiny. They felt they were meant to be a part of history, that they will be remembered for doing something very important.

There was a constant reference to our revolutionary history. As I noted earlier, one of the men planning to dynamite the Siskiyou Pass saw himself as a modern Paul Revere.

Keep in mind, members of the mob that stormed the Capitol on January 6th 2021, were yelling, "This is our 1776." Many people then and now are fulfilling a revolutionary identity that will give their life a higher purpose. They were seeking an opportunity to save the country from a threat we didn't perceive. Does this sound familiar?

Most of us don't think much about these right-wing activists. We may believe they are basically honorable American patriots who just happen to be just a bit overzealous. Then in 2021 there was a real political insurrection. This truly was a wake-up call for middle-America who earlier could not see any real problem with groups who carried the US flag and a gun.

To understand all the factors in this situation, it is necessary to consider the personal benefits that accrue to those persons involved in causes that are bigger than life. It's a pretty "heady" experience to take up arms in defense of your country while others are unaware that there's a danger. Under these circumstances they are the "Minute Men" that were warning the rest of us. These activists are propelled by a feeling of self-importance that few of us can appreciate.

Consider the thoughts of folks who came from all over the country to storm the Capitol building on January 6, 2021. They were volunteers who felt a purpose to take matters into their own hands. There was a feeling among them that they had no other choice but to "revolt." Many of them felt they were acting in our behalf. In their judgment there was nothing more important than saving "their country." While others were sitting at home watching TV, these self-appointed heroes felt a calling not unlike that of the four men who planned to dynamite the Siskiyou Pass.

We sometimes make the mistake of just condemning political violence by declaring the perpetrators were "wrong" in their goals and that they should be punished for disobeying the law. Some of us may simply view political violence as a law enforcement problem that doesn't concern us individually.

Instead, perhaps we should ask ourselves why there are thousands of people in our society who feel justified in taking up arms against established order? How has this idea been spread from coast to coast? Are cable-news and social media accountable for fermenting this cause? What are the names of elected officials who supported the Insurrection? Do we all bear some responsibility because we elected those officials? Can our democratic institutions survive continued armed insurrections?

The fate of our democracy may depend on your acceptance of a civic responsibility to take political action before it is too late.

THREE

Conspiratorial Thinking

P olitical stories based on fear and treachery are the ones folks love to repeat. At any given moment there are a string of fearful tales of impending doom being passed around the country. There's always a threat factor – a belief that there are some terrible people out there that want to do us harm. These stories may not be true, but there is evidence that they persuade a lot of us to be afraid.

Secret plots are tantalizing. It gives a lot of ordinary folks a chance to feel important as they tell nearly unbelievable stories that makes everyone feel like they are under a terrible threat. Bad news always drives out good news. It's always more interesting to hear about emerging forces that threaten our very survival. Competing stories about a rosy future are not even worth repeating. In recent years, there have been thousands (perhaps millions) of good, red-blooded Americans who are thirsty for threatening news. Currently the stories are more widespread because social media has become national in scope so stories from the one end of the continent can be heard at the other end within minutes. Facebook and cable news are here to stay. But federal and state authorities still don't seem to realize that propaganda is now communicated through the Internet. Looking back, January 6, 2021 shouldn't have been a surprise.

Early on I discovered that telling threatening stories was one of the main reasons why some folks get together. I knew an older woman in Medford that started out every conversation with me by saying, "Bill did you know that." She always had a fresh set of outlandish tales to tell me.

The way I stayed on good terms with her was to never question her accounts of political affairs. I always said, "Gosh, I didn't know that." For her and others like her, telling new stories became their reason for being.

Folks who heard and repeated these menacing stories were the real workhorses of political activism in southern Oregon. They were much more involved in politics than the leadership of either major political party. None of the people I knew on the extreme right or left ever spoke of being a Republican or Democrat. They looked down on local partisan organizations for not really understanding politics. Those on the far right and left thought the federal, state, and local officials had all been duped into believing that elections really mattered. Folks on the left-wing fringes were certain that there was an unseen, gigantic conspiracy of people behind the scene that were running American society, and they relished telling the stories that exposed the "true realities" of politics.

The most important ingredient for these conspiracy thinkers was "fear." The repeated allegation was that America was facing a deadly threat and that there was little time remaining before the takeover was complete. The assumption was that the opposition was gaining ground every day and that most of us were completely unaware. From this perspective, the situation was an emergency of epic proportions.

Conspiratorial thinking is common on both sides of the political spectrum, but right-wing tales were more interesting and creative. Some of these stories were dismissed by many as "so crazy that no one would believe them," but there is an audience out there that is eager to hear them.

Perhaps the best way to understand conspiratorial thinking is to relate an experience I had while attending a public meeting where rock music was presented as being a part of a Communist plot "take over America." There was a meeting in the old Medford Hotel on the subject of how a small group of Communists were using rock music to start an internal revolution. The presentation was given in the Rogue Room that had a floor-to-ceiling mirror covering the entire front wall of the room. I could sit in the front row listening to the speaker and look up at the mirror and see the faces of every other person in the room. It was an ideal atmosphere for hearing about the dangers of rock and roll, and watch the facial response of everyone else who had come to the meeting.

First the speaker made the case that rock musicians were left-wing people that have been trying to bring down our constitutional system for a long time. There was no disagreement on that point. Next, he made a quick reference to left-wing labor songs that fermented revolution, and finally he preceded to "hard rock," stating that our children were slowly being influenced by these "left-wing enemies of America." Then he described the "insidious tactics" being used by these musicians that were part of a Communist conspiracy to use that music to take over the country.

The speaker said that all rock music was composed with two hypnotic beats that were programmed into the mind of every young person in the country that listened to rock and roll. I noticed that everyone in the room nodded their heads to this unbelievable claim.

I wondered if any of them gave much critical thought to that charge? He then went on to say that these "beats" were included in every record listened to by the public.

But the shocking message came next.

It was the announcement that every Top-40 music radio station in the country had a secret recording of a third beat that would be played only when the Communists gave the order. The third beat was designed to mesh with the first two beats in a way that all the listeners would become helpless zombies willing to accept orders such as "Go out and dynamite the local National Guard armory" or "Do not obey your parents, teachers, or the local police."

I watched and listened to the presentation given to about eighty people who were hanging on to every word. The large up-front mirror showed every facial expression in the room. There were no disagreements voiced. No one said, "Prove it!" or "Give me an example." I did not see any expressions of doubt or any indication of disbelief. The whole conversion to believe in a Communist plot took less than one hour. Every face in the room looked convinced and worried. I was amazed at how quickly the crowd was convinced that there was a musical threat out there!

The questions were all about how they could expose this situation. Why weren't they told about this sooner? Would it help to call the radio station managers? Does the government know about this? Can we trust our own children? I could feel the anxiety level raise in the room. It had to be one of the most frightening stories these people had ever heard. I expect they couldn't wait to go back home and retell the tale. I wondered how their teenage grandchildren – who are rock fans – took the news?

I found that once people accept one conspiracy theory, it is very easy for them to accept a second and a third story. Conspiratorial thinking can become habitual. It can become a way of life. On some television channels, conspiracies grow like weeds. Folks line up every day to hear the new accounts of why you should be scared to death. I often wondered how the first version of each new tale got started. I'm sure there's a story behind every one of them.

In this particular case, nearly all the people in that room were more than fifty years old, and the message of rock music being a Communist plot meshed with their general annoyance of loud music that was so popular at the time. It seemed to make them feel better that the music they disliked was also a threat to the country. I wasn't the only person in the room taking notes. Many were writing it down, word for word.

The presentation that night was a complete success. I looked around and saw the faces of people who looked like they had something new to believe that would upset their lives. Someone stood by the door with an open container. It was like a religious event at a tent meeting. I noticed there were a lot of fives and tens in the bucket.

Later that night I started thinking that the meeting itself at the old Medford Hotel was itself like the "third beat" that made folks in that room turn into political zombies that would believe anything. Meetings like this opened a political door for the extreme right. Everyone in that room looked like they were powerless and afraid. The new found "fear" was palpable. Several expressed anger that elected officials had not warned them before. But perhaps the scariest thing from my perspective was: they could all vote.

When we hear about stories like the Communist plot to use rock music to take over the country, most of us laugh, thinking it is a fairy tale that no sensible person would believe. Then we may remember the more recent "big lie" told by Donald Trump about how he won the 2020 election. Which one of these stories was the biggest fairy tale no one would believe? What would you say? Actually, Trump's "big lie" had a lot more believers. By comparison the threat of rock music was just a sort of mid-range conspiracy theory.

The conspiracy stories of the 1960s and '70s were pretty innocent when compared to the stories of today. I don't recall any conspiracies of those times that resulted in loss of life. Folks could go around telling impossible tales and looking for Communists under their beds without creating a constitutional crisis. Today, however, the stories are literally threatening the body politic. Unbelievable stories are told that cause people to line up on opposing sides on nearly every issue. Also, this is the first time that right-wing groups have been encouraged by a former president, or current state governors and members of Congress. The conspiracies of today (unlike the earlier period) are a real threat to American democracy.

In the 1960s I remember thinking that the American people would someday becoming more sophisticated as time went on – that they would no longer be subject to repeating unbelievable political tales. Now I can see I was wrong, but I'm still not sure why.

FOUR

Paradise Lost in Wasco County

The largest utopian community in recent American history was established in 1981 near the small town of Antelope in eastern Oregon. Before the new folks arrived, there were only forty-six law-abiding people living in Antelope. Their secluded way of life changed dramatically as thousands of outsiders set up a commune just down the road.

The new settlement was started by a devoted group of religious followers of an Indian mystic and spiritual leader, Bhagwan Shree Rajnessh. The group bought the 64,000-acre Big Muddy River Ranch in northeast Oregon for $5.75 million, and in a few years, it was transformed into a city of 7,000 people with a growing infrastructure complete with its own police and fire departments, several restaurants, a crematorium, two hotels, a sewage treatment plant, a public transportation system, a 4,200 foot airstrip, and a post office with its own zip code, 92741. No one expected a new paradise would spring up in this part of Oregon.

The word spread to groups of visionary people all over the United States, Europe and Asia as they flocked to Rajneeshpuram to become a part of an exhilarating future. Some were certain it was the wave of the future, setting a standard that might be copied around the world. There was to be a place in northwestern America where complete freedom existed – where the "forbidden practices" of the old world were set aside in favor of a "brave new world." Sexual practices were to be relaxed and individuals could live up to their full potential in a loving atmosphere. Everyone would live in a communal society where all would share equally.

More than two-thirds of those who came to Rajneeshpuram were college graduates, many had advanced degrees. There was no shortage of people who spoke foreign languages. Some were PhDs, teachers, physicians, and attorneys along with thousands who were just looking for a new home. Surprisingly, many left their careers and came ready to build a community that featured state-of-the-art irrigation in a semi-desert climate. Organic food was plentiful as they tended vegetable gardens and planted trees around the ranch. Nearly everyone was dressed in simple clothing, colored light red and several shades of orange. Rank-and-file members felt equal as they built a society where everyone could feel secure.

But the first person I met from Rajneeshpuram didn't seem to be the product of a paradise on earth. She was a woman in her mid-thirties named Ma Anand Sheela (Sheela Silverman) who was the spokesperson for the movement. Sheela was an Indian-born, Swiss woman who was the power behind the throne. She was one of the most polarizing persons I have ever met. When she came to southern Oregon to recruit followers on campus, she went out of her way to use very abusive language. When challenged, she said Oregon officials who didn't like Rajneeshpuram "could go fuck themselves." She went on to say that she "didn't give a shit" what the students thought of her. It was difficult to understand the movement without remembering her leadership style. She was a lightning rod that clouded the entire movement and ultimately contributed to its downfall.

My wife and I visited Rajneeshpruram in its heyday and found it was many things to many people. First, it was a paradise for most of the residents, who seemed perfectly adjusted to practicing free love and following the teachings of their leader, "the Bhagwan" (the blessed one). Every day he drove one of his ninety-four Rolls-Royce cars through the compound as the residents cheered him. Bhagwan taught his followers to live in the moment, to share their earthly possessions and their bodies. He believed that individual freedom was achieved through free sexual expression. Nearly everyone I met had a smile on their face.

I talked to many people there, but I especially remember a woman from Switzerland who told me she had arranged to marry a US citizen at the ranch so she could become a legal American resident. According to her, she signed over a small fortune to the ranch. She met her "spouse to-be" briefly before the arranged marriage that was to grant her residential status in the United States. Another person I remember well was a retired high school teacher from Los Angeles who signed over his entire retirement income to the ranch in return for a "lifetime membership" in the commune. Each of them talked about the "joy" of being free of the repression of everyday life. Both were completely happy with their decisions and were certain that they would be happy for the rest of their days.

There were many television sets at Rajneeshpruram, but there was only one channel. It played lectures from Bhagwan twenty-four hours a day. He was never out of sight or out of mind. Even on television Bhagwan had a mystical quality. His eyes were unusually penetrating and he almost never blinked. There was a hypnotic quality in his presentation even though he seldom said anything he hadn't said many times before.

I was struck by the devotion everyone showed to Bhagwan. There was a full measure of affection in the air that followed him everywhere. At first, I thought the smiles and personal delight was just a façade, that he wasn't really loved by everyone, but later I could see it was genuine. Every afternoon his followers lined the street waiting for him to drive by in his Rolls Royce. The only thing I could compare it to was the atmosphere in a spontaneous church situation where people were seized by the holy spirit that caused them to dance and shake. There was an unbridled joy that seemed to be catching. I don't remember ever seeing this many people, this happy, greeting an old man who was parading through the streets.

If you had an ounce of idealism in you, it would have been easy to join in and throw caution to the wind. It was "heaven on earth" and easy to join. The 7,000 followers had everything they wanted and they were certain that they were permanently "sheltered" from the rest of society. Even though the movement was just a few years old, there was a felling in the air that it would last forever. The fact that the movement was international added to its authenticity. It was real, and it was located right here in the middle of Wasco County, Oregon.

There were nightly meditation sessions in a large canvas-covered building that housed 4,000 people. The half-hour sessions featured complete silence which gave me a mind-altering experience. Thousands of folks sat on the floor for 30-minutes without making a sound. I was afraid I was going to sneeze. It was easy to forget that eastern Oregon was a very conservative region where there were more guns than people. But for the time being the commune was an other-worldly paradise where everyone seemed happy.

There was a whole new sense of trust among these folks. I did not see locks on any doors or on the hundreds of bicycles that were parked everywhere. It appeared to be in another era where everyone was expected to love each other. The community was a huge concentration of left-wing folks who seemed unconcerned with the outside world. As I said before, everyone was smiling.

But there was another world that was just outside the perimeter of the compound that nearly everyone seemed to ignore. When we entered the ranch, we noticed guard towers manned by men with semi-automatic weapons and high-powered rifles. Police inside the commune were armed with automatic weapons. Strangely, I felt like my wife and I were the only ones who noticed how many guns there were in the compound.

One of the conditions I agreed to in visiting Rajneeshpuram was to surrender my car and its keys with the promise that they would be returned when we were ready to leave. My wife and I were also required to register with a clerk and state our addresses and occupations. My wife was an insurance agent and she abbreviated her occupation as "INS Agent." Later we were certain that this was misinterpreted by the clerk to mean Immigration and Naturalization Service because we were immediately given very special treatment. We were assigned to a room at the far end of the Zen Hotel with a visible microphone hanging from the ceiling. We were sure our conversations were listened to by the staff. With a bit of humor in our voices as we kept saying in loud voices, "It sure is nice here. I really do like the Bhagwan, don't you?" Later we found out that many rooms in the hotel were bugged.

As visitors, we were charged $120 a day which included our

bugged room, three meals and free rein to roam around the commune. We were given a map of the entire city, complete with the Walt Whitman Grove and the Alan Watts Canyon. It was a truly international atmosphere with people from all over the world. Everyone made eye contact easily with a ready smile. Many seemed to feel right at home whether working in the fields or sitting in one of the restaurants. The food and conversations were excellent. It was an interesting place to meet and talk to a wide variety of people from all over the world.

But Rajneeshpuram was an obvious contradiction. It was a place of complete freedom with all the trappings of an armed camp. All of the "security" was said to be for the protection of the residents, to keep out other nearby Oregonians who were not happy with the attempt to take over the local county. From the start, the Rajneeshees did not get along with their eastern Oregon neighbors. There were a lot of local folks who felt threatened by the influx of all these "new Oregonians" dressed in red and orange.

Early on the Rajneesh leaders decided to enter local politics. There was a struggle to register enough voters at the ranch to win an election and take political control of Wasco County. To this end, Rajneesh leaders bussed in approximately 4,000 homeless people from around the country and registered them to vote. Next the communal leaders came up with a scheme to decrease the voter turnout of longtime Wasco County residents on Election Day by lacing 10 salad bars in nearby towns with a salsa that contained salmonella. More than 700 local residents were infected. There were no fatalities, but forty-five people were hospitalized. It turned out that the ideal life on the ranch was going on inside a bubble. The question was: how long would the bubble last?

In addition to the salmonella poisoning, several other allegations surfaced. Arson was suspected when the Wasco County Planning Department Office was set on fire, destroying files involving the Rajneeshees. It was also revealed that several Rajneeshees had a "hit list" to "take out" several Oregonians who were not cooperative. According to insiders, there were plans to assassinate Charles Turner, the United States Attorney for Oregon, and Dave Frohnmayer, the Oregon Attorney General. When faced by Oregon officials, Ma Anand Sheela became more aggressive in her statements to the press. Perhaps her biggest mistake was to increase the armed force to defend the commune. Public opinion across Oregon quickly reflected a negative view on what was going on in Rajneeshpuram.

The government reaction was immediate after the guns came out and the poisoning episode was discovered. Within days, federal and state officials descended on Rajneeshpruram. The Oregon Attorney General charged that Rajneeshpuram was a religious community that violated the principle of separation of church and state. Enforcers of Oregon environmental laws charged that the Rajneeshees had converted rural lands to urban use without going through the correct procedures. Immigration and naturalization officials charged that federal laws had been violated by so-called "marriages of convenience." Arrests and deportation orders followed quickly.

It was not long before the Bhagwan and several leaders fled in two Lear Jets. They were arrested when the planes landed in North Carolina. Back at the ranch there was confusion and uncertainty. People began leaving as the authorities moved in, but it was a long road back to where they had come from. Folks hitched-hiked out of Rajneeshpuram in all directions.

All the "paraphernalia of paradise" was put up for sale. It wasn't long before there was an auction on all the earth-moving and farm equipment left behind. The Bhagwan's Rolls Royces were put up for sale and purchased by a dealer in Texas. During the dark, dreary days of an Oregon winter, the paradise was dissolving before our eyes. It was a very unceremonious ending for an international community where everyone was expected to be completely free.

Negative media coverage of Rajneeshpuram was a key factor. At the beginning there were non-critical television pictures of hundreds of people all dressed in red and orange throwing up their arms gleefully as Bhagwan drove by in one of his Rolls Royce cars. The implication was that these folks were child-like people who were possibly brain-washed. Next came the grainy films of sexual orgies implying that the whole operation was a kinky nightmare. After that were the pictures of expensive farm equipment, luxury cars, and new buildings suggesting there was an unlimited supply of wealth and economic power. As relations with other Oregonians deteriorated, there was more talk about the number of guns in the commune. Toward the end, there were TV pictures of Rajneeshees on the firing range practicing their marksmanship for a probable invasion of state and federal military forces. One newspaper report concluded that there was more fire power at Rajneeshpuram than with all the police forces in Oregon combined.

The media account of the commune started with an almost unbelievable example of the naiveté of the chanting people all dressed alike, and it progressed steadily downward to include sexually immoral activities, illegal practices, and finally a threatening political situation that had to be rooted out. Much of the blame for the disastrous public relations went to Ma Anand Sheela (Sheela Silverman) who seemed to enjoy the role of being a power-mad woman who thought she was above the law. One unconfirmed report I heard was that she got so angry that she wanted to have a Rajneeshpuram airplane drop a home-made bomb on the Wasco County Courthouse.

As time went on, she was exposed and blamed by Bhagwan as the reason why local, state, and federal officials were closing in on the commune. It was a crushing end for the thousands of people that lived there, and it all happened so fast. No one expected Rajneeshpuram would rise and fall so quickly. The people I met thought the commune would last "forever." That was just a few months before everything collapsed.

The life-long plans for the communal residents were cut short as state and federal agents moved in and took control. Many tears were shed by the mostly young people in red and orange clothes as they left the ranch. Soon after, there were lots of used, colored clothes in local secondhand clothing stores.

The folks that left Rajneeshpuram had a lot of questions that related to what had happened: Was the commune destined to fail before it started? Could a "perfect world" be built where there was complete equality? If everyone was living in harmony, why were there so many guns around? Why couldn't the leaders of the Rajneesh Movement live in harmony with their Oregon neighbors? Who decided they could openly violate federal and state laws? Why didn't someone persuade Ma Anand Sheela that you can never win a political fight in the United States by threatening to use lethal force against state and federal governmental officials?

In retrospect, the whole idea was very amateurish. A group of students from my upper division political science classes could have come up with a better plan. They should have hired a political consultant who knew the law. Anyone who was aware if Oregon zoning laws would have concluded that you couldn't violate all those laws with the expectation that everything would turn out well. The vision of a paradise on earth may have been attractive to many, but the leadership did not have the political abilities to make it come true.

On the human level, Rajneeshpuram was a disaster. It raised the expectations of thousands who were left behind to contemplate "what could have been." There was an overwhelming feeling of a heartbreaking let-down for the folks who expected to find heaven on earth.

It hasn't happened yet, but some keep on trying.

FIVE

Raising the Flag on Campus

F our unarmed college students were shot to death by members of the Ohio National Guard while protesting the Vietnam War. The campus of Kent State University had become a killing field on May 4, 1970. The entire incident was filmed and broadcast on national television news. Within hours, students across the country turned out in anger and threatened to close down college campuses coast to coast.

It was mid-day when news from Kent State reached Southern Oregon College. There was an immediate student demand to cancel classes in respect for those who had been killed and wounded. Soon there was a spontaneous gathering in the college auditorium where the president of the student body demanded that the campus be closed down and then – after a lot of shouting – the majority insisted that the City of Ashland should be shut down, as well. In addition, there was a voice vote to organize a candle-light march that evening through Ashland to Lithia Park in the center of the city. Emotions were running high all afternoon as everyone pre-pared for the march.

Late in the afternoon I spoke to a deputy from the Jackson County Sheriff Office who said they had received reports from folks outside of Ashland that there was to be an armed convoy of local folks that would take steps to keep the city open. The sheriff's deputy told me I should inform the students that, if there was any shooting, they should all lie down on the street so the law enforcement folks would know that the only people standing were "the trouble-makers." I passed on word to the students as they were preparing to march down Siskiyou Boulevard into downtown Ashland. The emotions of the student body were raised even higher. One student told me that she had "never been involved in something like this before." Nearly everyone in the throng of students had a candle. There was a lot of anxiety and small talk about what they could expect during the candle-light march.

Hundreds of townspeople lined Siskiyou Boulevard as a group of approximately 150 students marched in candle-light silence. The killings at Kent State had happened only hours before, but the students had already made a heart-felt commitment. We didn't see any guns, but there were a lot of police officers standing along the street. The tension in the air was palpable. Students around me were weeping softly. When we arrived at Lithia Park there was another rally called by the student body president. A collective decision was made that students would gather again tomorrow morning at 8:00 a.m. on the campus in front of Churchill Hall to lower the American flag to half-mast.

I arrived near the flagpole shortly after 7:30 am. The most noticeable thing was the number of pickup trucks parked across the street with groups of men who didn't look like students. There were also two police cars parked in a no-parking zone. Word had traveled through the crowd that this was going to be a standoff. The guys across the street pledged that the flag was going up as usual and the students were standing firm around their plan to lower the flag to half-mast.

It seemed like a long time before a maintenance worker came out with the flag tucked under his arm. There was dead silence on both sides of the street. I remember feeling tense as the flag was hooked to the rope. They came the surprise! The rope wouldn't move! It was caught on something. Every eye was riveted on a flag that couldn't be raised. I then noticed that the pulley on the pole had been smashed, perhaps by a hammer. At any rate there was no way to raise the flag. At this point, everyone wanted to see the broken pulley. Even some of the guys across the street came over to inspect the damage. The students were confused and not sure of what to do next. There was a lot of nervous laughter. The stand-off had been averted.

Again, I noticed tears in the eyes of some students, but there were also smiles and a sense of relief. There hadn't been any violence. The men in the pickup trucks drove away within fifteen minutes. The police stayed a little longer. The maintenance man took the flag back inside Churchill Hall. But then everyone started to wonder who had broken the pulley.

Several days later word leaked out that two of the maintenance men had taken it upon themselves to smash the pulley. There were no college officials involved. As far as I know, two state employees talked it over and decided to save us all from ourselves. The maintenance men became unsung campus heroes. The next day the flag was flying again at full-mast.

The incident lingered in the form of the impact it had on individual students. One by one I heard young people say they felt as though they had gone through an initiation process whereby, for the first times in their lives, they had taken a risk to stand up for something they believed in. That may have been a noble experience, but looking back, I could see that it was a two-edged sword because the whole episode demonstrated how vulnerable we were to political tensions that could spread like wild fire. The whole event ended with an "accident" that really did save us from ourselves.

If it had not of been for a broken pulley, the flag pole incident might have turned into another case of unexpected violence that flared out of control. Sometimes a few people behind the scene can free us from a dangerous situation we have created. In retrospect, it seems irrational that lives could have been lost because of raising or lowering a cloth symbol on a flag pole.

This was a case when people were willing to put their lives on the line with little information about an event that happened thousands of miles away. It was an example of how fast the veneer of public order can be ripped away when politics are involved. It demonstrated again that there are often underground actions taken by unseen figures that shape a political outcome. Unknown to me at the time, there was to be more of this to come in just a few more months.

SIX

"Vortex 1" at McIver Park

O nly in Oregon would the governor sponsor a rock concert to avert expected political violence. It was all kind of informal, but the word on the street was that the state police would turn a blind eye to drug use and nudity at a rock festival in a remote area organized by the state government if the young people involved didn't join a riot that was anticipated to take place twenty-five miles away in downtown Portland.

The 52nd National Convention of the American Legion was to be held in Portland, Oregon, from August 29 through September 3, 1970. More than 25,000 legionnaires were expected to attend and President Richard Nixon was to be the keynote speaker. There would to be marching bands, decorated floats, and many columns of parading veterans from every state in the union. Portland was to be decked out in banners and flags, with patriotic buntings adorning the light poles.

But a group of local young people decided that they would hold an alternate public "convention" on the streets of Portland to publicize their opposition to US involvement in the Vietnam War.

Word soon spread to radical groups around the nation to join in to what was to be called the People's Army Jamboree (PAJ).

At be beginning, there was a pledge from both sides that the two events would be peaceful, but soon there were fears that there might be violence to match or exceed the clash between antiwar protesters and the Chicago police just two years earlier at the 1968 Democratic Convention. It was a scary thought for city leaders. Downtown merchants in Portland began to prepare by boarding up store fronts and making plans to defend business locations from the expected violence.

Oregon Governor Tom McCall was also concerned. He was a progressive Republican who had been a journalist, but he was also a veteran and his son was currently serving in Vietnam, so he refused to take sides on the issue. But McCall knew the state was ill-prepared for the expected clash. The FBI had warned him that up to 50,000 protestors were expected to disrupt the convention. In a crisis atmosphere, McCall and his staff huddled together with outside groups to find a way to avert the impending crisis.

A loosely formed, peaceful, counter-culture group in Portland met with McCall's Chief of Staff, Ed Westerdahl. They jointly proposed that the state should sponsor a rock festival twenty-five miles outside of Portland during the same period of the convention to "drain off" young people that might join the PAJ. It seemed like a far-fetched idea to trick the protestors, but no one could think of anything else except hunkering down for a battle that might cost many lives and considerable property damage. The pressure was on, the state government had to do something.

McCall's first response to the state-sponsored rock festival idea was not favorable. Reportedly he shouted, "Westerdahl, you're crazy," but the more information he had on the probable consequences, the better the outrages idea sounded. The staff said McCall consented with a "lot of reservations." He was worried there would be a devastating clash in Portland, but no one could come up with a better idea to avert the expected violence.

It was decided that the festival, "Vortex 1," would be held in Milo McIver State Park, a remote box-canyon area with one way in and no other routes out. It would be fairly easy to block anyone who tried to leave the park. The plan was to let folks in with a strong "encouragement" to stay for four days. From the very beginning there was an "understanding" that the state would turn a blind eye to drug use and nudity. The expectation was that young folks could pretty much do anything they wanted just so they didn't go back into downtown Portland. The word soon spread around the area to attend the rock festival as young people looked on the map to find McIver Park.

The Clackamas River flowed through the park so there was going to be plenty of opportunity for skinny dipping and mud baths. A stage was built by state workers for rock bands – yoga classes were scheduled – "Peace in Vietnam" teach-ins were to take place – a free clinic for drug overdoses was provided – there was an information booth for lost children – and free food was served compliments of local organic restaurants. Everything was done to make Vortex 1 user-friendly. There was an open invitation to come to Vortex 1 for a relaxing break from life.

Early on there was an announcement that big-name bands like Jefferson Airplane and the Grateful Dead were to perform. There was talk that Vortex 1 might be like the iconic "Woodstock" that had taken place one year earlier in New York state. In the end the big bands didn't show up, but local bands were more than willing to provide rock music for the approximately 30,000 young people that flocked to Vortex 1. There was a long traffic jam that reached back into the suburbs of Portland. The word on the street was that folks could get away with almost anything as long as it was peaceful.

The press called it "the Governor's Pot Party." There were mixed feelings around the state about permitting the law to be broken in full sight of the state police. Nothing like this had ever been tried before in American history. Was it brilliant or was it absolutely stupid? Folks in rural areas thought the governor had sold out – that he was being soft on enforcing the law. The question in everyone's mind was whether it was worth holding a state-sponsored rock festival to avert violence. One elderly woman on TV disagreed. She thought the governor should "shoot the protestors" and "not give in to the trouble-makers." Other people, however, thought it was the most "creative idea they'd ever heard to avoid violence." After it ended, most Oregonians thought it was a master stroke to save Portland from what appeared to be certain disaster.

During this whole period, I was in downtown Portland working as a part-time journalist for the *Medford Mail Tribune*. In the beginning there were only a few hundred protestors. I asked one of the leaders about his estimate of 50,000 protestors that were coming into Portland. He told me the press had said 25,000 legionnaires were expected so he "just doubled the number and "pulled the 50,000 number out of his hat." The FBI quoted that number to everyone. So, the story of 50,000 radicals invading Portland was based on a made-up number. In truth it was difficult to estimate the number of protestors because many of them were scattered around in different parts of the city. The estimate was that only about 1,500 actually showed up to demonstrate downtown.

But the situation in Portland was tense despite the fact that many young people had been diverted to McIver State Park, twenty-five miles away. There was widespread grumbling among the PAJ about the young people who chose to go to the park rather than confront the American Legion.

The idea that folks could "do anything" at Vortex 1 was tantalizing to an unexpected group in Portland. There was a group of about thirty legionnaires who reportedly said, "The hell with the convention, we want to see what's happening at Vortex 1."

The People's Army Jamboree that showed up in Portland was a disorganized group made up many non-violent hippies with a sprinkling of hard-core revolutionaries who intended on causing a violent confrontation. The hard-core members were eager to talk with me in hopes I would write a newspaper story about their plans. One guy from northern California showed me a box full of oven cleaner that he was going to spray in the eyes of the police. He had hopes of turning the convention into a full-scale bloody riot with disabled police officers sent to the hospital.

The first gathering of PAJ was in Lair Hill Park, a small clearing just a few blocks from the downtown area, but Portland police were in the process of moving everyone to Delta Park, a larger wide-open area several miles north of the downtown area along the Columbia River. The police tried to convince the protestors they would have more room to be comfortable, but in fact they were being removed to keep them away far from the downtown. The city and state officials were trying to set up a situation where everyone's constitutional rights were protected in an atmosphere that minimized the chance of a violent confrontation. It was surprising that the PAJ consented to the move. They were stranded several miles out of the city as the convention celebration went on as planned downtown. The only way to get downtown was to take a city bus. There was something kind of unbelievable about hordes of armed revolutionaries taking a city bus downtown so they can start a riot.

On the second day of the American Legion Convention, I was in an elevator at the Portland Hilton Hotel and by chance I pressed the sub-basement level. When the elevator door opened, I saw several hundred members of the Oregon National Guard dressed in riot gear ready to go. I was told, "You can't come in here." This was another example of putting both the PAJ and the National Guard out of site so the convention could go with a minimum of tensions.

There was also a concern that Richard Nixon would add to the hostile drama out on the street. But Oregon officials convinced the White House that Nixon would add to the problem of keeping order. As a result, Nixon announced he was too busy and he decided to send Vice President Spiro Agnew to Portland in his place. (This was before Agnew had become such a polarizing figure.) Agnew's speech inside the convention was generally non-controversial by design.

Outside the convention center, opposing parades were kept apart so angry comments were usually far away. Members of the PAJ chanted "1-2-3-4, we don't want your fucking war," but it didn't seem to be shouted in anger. There was a large sign, "Stop the Killing" that sorted of blended in with the American flags and bunting. The oven cleaner was nowhere to be seen and there was no hint of real danger as parents and children were out on the sidewalk watching the parade. According to the Portland police, one window in the downtown was broken. The cost for repair was about $40.

The American Legion parade itself was rather boring. There were thousands of marching legionnaires wearing military uniforms that were too tight for them. Some of the band music was out of tune. The network TV crews that expected a riot seemed a bit disappointed.

In the end, the kids had a free rock festival, the National Guard stayed in the basement, the PAJ was scattered outside the city, Nixon stayed home, and to the surprise of nearly everyone, Portland was spared from destruction. It was quite a spectacle for everyone involved.

Tom McCall had been worried during this whole period because he was up for re-election two months after the convention. He had told the press that he feared he had just "committed political suicide" by launching Vortex 1. But to his surprise, the governor's standing went up in the polls. In November McCall defeated his Democratic opponent in November by a significant margin.

Vortex 1 was the kind of political maneuver a governor can only do once. It was a risky underground move. It may actually have been illegal. Some editorial writers thought it was a bit dishonest to distract the young people with a free rock concert. McCall's opponents criticized him for manipulated the protestors, but that was a minority point of view.

There developed a kind of mythology surrounding Vortex 1. Supporters of the governor concluded that McCall may have saved many lives – that he may have avoided an untold amount of private property destruction. But folks that went to Vortex 1 told a slightly different story. The reports from the park were that nearly all the young people there were local and rather nonpolitical; they were attracted to the "relaxed atmosphere" at McIver Park. Press interviews in the park showed that many of them didn't know much about the American Legion Convention and didn't really care. It seemed unlikely that these young people would have been violent protestors if Vortex 1 had not taken place. At the end of the day, the fear of widespread violence was probably unfounded. But it was one hell of a show, both inside and outside the city.

Looking back, it seems that launching Vortex 1 was an exceptionally lucky decision made by Governor McCall that could have backfired. But maybe violence was averted because nearly everyone felt that Vortex 1 was a brilliant move that was bound to succeed. At the end of the day, there was a belief out on the street that it was necessary to take extra ordinary measures to save Portland from the "50,000 revolutionaries" who were expected to show up. The major players thought the governor had performed "political magic" by redirecting the young people to a spot twenty-five miles out of town. Tom McCall became something like the "Pied Piper of Oregon" as he led 30,000 young people into a box canyon where they became harmless.

In truth, Vortex 1 probably succeeded because people (when faced by what seemed to be certain violence) wanted to believe in an ingenious political tactic that no one had ever tried before. It was an outrageous move for a governor to set up a situation where everyone could break the law in order to keep the peace.

In the end, Vortex 1 appealed to everyone because it was a great political story that everyone could enjoy. It was also the ultimate case of underground politics succeeding. But it's interesting there's not been a "Vortex 2."

SEVEN

Presidents in the Eyes of Children

One of the most important political events of my childhood was the installation of our indoor plumbing. It was big news when we were told that we were going to be hooked up to the city sewer system. One of my earliest memories was standing near a deep ditch in our front yard looking down at the black sewer pipes that were being connected by men from the WPA (Works Project Administration). I spent several days watching these men, hired by the federal government, dig the ditch by hand. It was quite an event for a four-year-old to ask every day when it would be finished. I was really excited.

One evening, after the WPA men had left for the day, I stood there with my father looking down at the black pipes that would soon be connected and covered over with dirt. I asked him who had sent the men to dig the ditch and put in our toilet. My dad brought the project down to my level and said Franklin Roosevelt had sent in the crew to "help us get an indoor toilet." I asked more questions about Roosevelt and found out he didn't live nearby, but that he was our "friend."

That was enough for me. The conversation finally cleared up the subject in my mind by giving me a name. I now had someone that I felt was responsible for our new facility. It may sound unbelievable, but I remember mentally thanking the president every time I flushed the toilet. It was my first political memory. It gave me an example that government could do "good things."

There was another experience that I remembered involving my mother, who had all sorts of magazines around the house. I recall a conversation she had at the dinner table about an article she read about Frances Perkins who was Roosevelt's Secretary of Labor. She said Perkins was credited with influencing the president on reform issues that would benefit average people. According to this article, Perkins convinced Roosevelt he should propose the Social Security Administration that became law in 1935, the year I was born.

This discussion about Frances Perkins took place when I was about seven or eight years old. I remember one thing my mother said, she thought the Frances Perkins had thought up ways "to help people." Again, the message was a positive one, and it was at my level to understand.

There were all sorts of stories going around my family about the Roosevelt Administration and how much they were involved in helping ordinary people. My older brother told me about messenger boys in Washington, D.C., that rode bicycles between the White House and the Capitol carrying bundles of messages back and forth. My brother said that some of the bicycles were old and worn out, and kids like us could get them free if we wrote to the president. He said he heard on the radio about a boy who wrote the president saying he was poor and couldn't afford a bicycle, and could the president send him one of the old bicycles no one wanted?

According to my brother, the boy received a brand-new bicycle from Montgomery Wards a few weeks later. It came along with a personal note signed by Franklin Roosevelt. We thought about writing to the president, but we never did.

I continued to personalize the President during World War II. I had an image in my mind of him sending American troops into battle. I didn't know the details of the war, but I knew he was the man in charge. The bottom line was that he cared about us, that he was doing all he could to protect us from the enemy. I thought he must care about kids like me.

My personal view of the President was the main reason why his death in April of 1945 hit me so hard. I was just nine years old and I was walking home from school when I passed our next-door neighbor woman who was sitting on her front porch just gazing out at the street. She was in tears so I went up on the porch and asked if I could do anything to help her. She turned to me and touched me on the shoulder and said, "The President is dead. What will we do now?" I didn't know what to say. He was like the father of our country, the person we could depend on, and now he was gone. I recall that his replacement, Harry Truman, didn't give me the assurance I needed. For some reason Truman wasn't much of a father figure in my mind.

But my dad knew a guy who was a big Truman fan. It was 1948 and Truman was running behind in the polls in his re-election campaign. His Republican opponent, Thomas Dewey, was a very capable man who had a reputation of being a crime fighter while serving as governor of New York state. This friend of my father came up with a scheme to help Truman win by visiting several taverns in our area. He loved to talk about politics, and when he found a Dewey voter, he would make a personal proposal. The

Truman supporter said he was going to be out of town on election day and he wouldn't be able to vote for the President. He asked the Dewey voter if he would stay home that day so his non-vote would be balanced out. My dad's friend said his proposal "worked like a charm." He claimed he made his deal with twelve people before election day and then he went out and voted for Truman. He said he couldn't take credit for the entire state, but he could take a "good part of the credit" for Truman winning our county.

Up through my teenage years I got a pretty heavy dose of Democrats in my political socialization process, but I was to have a personal contact with a Republican leader that left a very favorable impression. I graduated from high school in 1953 and got a summer job as a bellhop at State Game Lodge in the Black Hills of South Dakota. The Game Lodge was known as "The Summer White House" because Calvin Coolidge had stayed there for several months during the summer of 1927. And as luck would have it, another president was going to visit the Lodge in June of 1953, which was my second month as a bellhop.

President Dwight Eisenhower was to visit the Lodge for three days on June 11-13 of 1953. On his arrival in South Dakota, he first dedicated Ellsworth Air Force Base in Rapid City, and then drove out the Game Lodge to do some fishing. Everyone was nervous as we could hear the secret service chatter about the President being ten miles out, five miles out, and finally his motorcade pulled in out front of the Lodge. It was one of those moments when you actually see a famous person walk into view. You couldn't believe it, but it was really him. In Eisenhower's case, he was all smiles as he shook our hands and made small talk in the hotel lobby. After a few minutes he excused himself to go up to his room to freshen up before he went out to try his luck in a trout stream nearby.

I was the bellhop on duty when a call came down from the President's room for a bucket of ice. As I walked up the grand staircase, I was certain that the secret service men would take the ice from me, but they didn't. Some of them were advance men that I had met during the past week. I had gotten to know them pretty well during that week. The secret service men all called me by first name and waved me on as I approached the door of Room 36, the Presidential Suite.

When I knocked on the door, I heard a voice say, "Come in." It was his valet, who was standing to my right folding pants over a hanger. He motioned for me to put the ice down, but as I was walking over to a small table, I looked to my left as the President came out of the bedroom carrying a towel. He had just taken a shower and he was standing there in the nude. I was careful to look him in the eye and not look below the waist. He spoke to me first asking where I was from. I told him about my home town. His reply was "That's a great place for trout fishing, isn't it?" I said, "Yes, Mr. President." I was speechless, I couldn't think of anything more to say. I just stood there frozen, a seventeen-year-old kid just off the farm with the President of the United States who had no clothes on. He finally broke the silence and said, "Just put the ice down over there." I said, "Yes, Mr. President," as I backed out of the room.

No one on the Game Lodge staff would believe me. They kept saying, "He wouldn't do that. He would have at least put the towel around his waist." It wasn't until I was in the US Army that I realized that military men do not stand on formality. If a military man is with other men, the towel around the waist is optional.

Afterwards, I started thinking about the casual nature of Dwight Eisenhower – what an easy going, friendly person he was. He did his best to make everyone feel as ease, especially me. At that moment in time, he was perhaps the most famous man in the world, and certainly the most powerful, but he was completely secure and comfortable in his role. The majority opinion at the Game Lodge was that he was a lot easier to take care of him than the new rich that we saw frequently. I learned a lot that summer about people who were secure in their place like the President, versus the others who just wanted to impress the hotel staff.

Later, when I was in graduate school, I did an interview by mail with Eisenhower on my dissertation topic, Presidential Campaigning in Presidential Elections. My questions concerned his involvement in congressional campaigns. I found him to be just as cordial and helpful as he had been that day in the State Game Lodge. I had a new hero!

Years later I always thought of him in a special way, I jokingly told my friends, "The President had nothing to hide from me."

EIGHT

Politics of the '60s

When I arrived in the Rogue Valley in 1964, I didn't realize that the whole country was about to go through a reaction to the Civil Rights Act of that year. The measure prohibited racial segregation in public places and banned discrimination based on race, religion, gender, or national origin. It was used as an instrument to enforce integration throughout the country. But the importance noted here is that the opponents and proponents of that law set a new standard of thinking and behaving in politics. Our politics would never be the same again after the 1960s.

It is now clear that enactment of that law began a chain reaction that affected folks in every other part of the country. The upcoming series of events of the 1960s left an indelible mark on our political behavior. It changed how we see our adversaries and how we see ourselves. Much of the division we feel today has its roots in the 1960s.

My political orientation on tactics was established before the 1960s. I was wedded to the two-party system and the mantra, "work through the system." One of the first things I did when I arrived on campus was to reenergize two campus political organizations: the

Young Democrats and the Young Republicans. I made certain that both of them would have a faculty advisor who would encourage political participation through the regular political channels.

A turning point in that process occurred one day as I ran into one of my students on campus who had been a member of the Young Democrats. I asked why he had not been coming to meetings. He told me of his new interest in an organization called Students for a Democratic Society (SDS). He said this new radical group founded at the University of Michigan was more relevant to his political views. He said they didn't just talk about politics – they actually went out on the street and did something. This particular student later took a leadership role in the campus SDS chapter. He was deeply involved in the anti-war movement that swept the country during the next ten years. I'm pretty sure he never returned to the Democratic Party.

Soon after I had another student who told me that he was interested in a new conservative organization on campus called the Young Americans for Freedom (YAF). He said it had been founded by William F. Buckley, a noted libertarian and conservative, and was much more active for young people than the old Republican Party. This student said he was dropping his membership in the Young Republicans. Later, that student moved to Portland where he continued his involvement in right-wing politics. I doubt he ever came back to the Republican Party.

These two students were really pathfinders on campus leading others into a more activist brand of politics. Both the SDS and YAF were formed in 1960 and they each had a strong following by the mid-1960s. When I arrived on the scene, college students were in the process of departing from the formal political parties to more activist organizations. In a real sense, the students were out in front of me in terms of political tactics. They were learning the new street politics that were sweeping the nation.

After the mid-1960s, many White folks in the American South and other parts of the nation felt their backs were up against the wall. They developed a method of fighting back against the Civil Rights Act of 1964 with unparalleled intensity. It ranged from using the legal process to the illegal methods of clandestine repression. Some leaders resisted by "standing in the school house door," but there were others that set off a bomb that killed four little girls in the largest Black church in Birmingham, Alabama.

Much of what right-wing groups do today to resist change was patterned after the methods developed in the 1960s. It was the politics of confrontation, using any and all means to hold the line and block change. It established an aggressive version of defensive politics on the right that we see imitated later all over the country. Activists on the extreme right no longer just traded stories in the backroom. They went out on the street in front of the Supreme Court, or in more intensive moments, they put on white robes and paraded down Main Street.

The nation also learned a method of politics from left-wing protestors who intentionally challenged segregation practices. There was a feeling of righteousness as Black and White folks alike risked their lives assaulting the state and local power structures. Jim Crow laws were their target and street actions were their strategy. Tactics ranged from peaceful, non-violent marches to rioting and the destruction of property. The activists invoked a sense of moral outrage as they persuaded others to follow their lead. These were the risen people who defied the law. This method established a pattern we see today with marches, and the threat of street violence.

Activist of the left and right also learned how to use the media.

For the first time, television was used not only to inform the public, but to politicize the conflict on both sides. From the comfort of their own homes, everyone saw police dogs biting Black children – they saw the arrogant behavior of the local sheriffs, and they also observed unarmed protestors who marched into a wall of state troopers on horses armed with clubs. Everyone saw hometown folks objecting to the National Guard forcing integration in their schools, and hooded members of the Ku Klux Klan marching through the streets. More recently, social media has been added to the ability to get noticed politically. Televeision has forever changed the way we think and act in politics.

It wasn't realized it at the time, but the tactics used on both sides in the 1960s set off a series of changes that showed up again and again. Street confrontations became more common. More people started carrying placards. Singing and marching became a more important part of street politics. Folks all over the country came to realize that protesting for or against an issue could bring quick results. People without power recognized they could band together to press for change. And on the other side, those who resisted change developed methods of organizing to hold the line. Short, crisp interviews with the both sides became a standard part of the TV broadcast.

The old idea of working through the system no longer had the same appeal. Writing letters to the editor and holding town meetings was too slow. The visual effect of television short-circuited the political process. A small dramatic, televised protest today could fill the public square tomorrow. The cat was out of the bag – direct action out on the street could bring results quicker than signing petitions. Everyone learned a new way to conduct themselves in the political world. There was no going back to quieter times.

It was only a matter of time before a larger segment of the electorate caught on to how to use the new brand of televised politics. Field workers in Oregon and California sang songs as they organized in the fields and won union contracts. Evangelical Christians came out of their churches and chanted in front of the Supreme Court building. LGBTQ folks, who had been in the closet, came out to parade down Main Street with the rainbow flag. Opposition to the war in Vietnam grew as campus protests was televised. Everyone knew what the Tea Party stood for because they saw them on television. School shootings and gun issues brought out people on both sides. Opponents of immigration policy paraded along the border. Women across the country organized the largest street demonstrations to date. The question on whether to take the Covid-19 vaccine was played out on TV. School board meetings became the scene for violent confrontations as parents insisted the curriculum be changed to reflect more conservative views. Social media gave us more fictitious reasons to hate each other. The list went on and on. Politics became more dramatic and more visual. Few people recognized that nearly all of our new behavior came out of the 1960s.

Political, social, racial, economic, religious, and cultural organizers have learned it is important to do a press release before a demonstration so they can gain maximum coverage. Political tactics are planned to fit the media opportunities. Activist groups learned to schedule street demonstrations to meet a deadline for the evening news. Now cable TV networks need to fill a twenty-four-hour news cycle and activists are willing to give them dramatic pictures any time of the day. There is no going back to a time when politics (for most people) was confined to voting.

Before this new activism, there was an unwritten rule that

respectable political groups should confine themselves to a positive message – that they should say what they were for rather than what they were against. It soon became apparent that it was more newsworthy to show what was wrong rather than what was right. Television editors focused on short, dramatic statements that sharpened news coverage. Political leaders learned how to speak in 30 second sound bites that would tell their story and increase viewer interest. Television cameras loved to show sweating migrant workers that were exploited and treated like modern slaves – TV could flash pictures of defenseless Viet Cong sympathizers being beaten by American soldiers – the evening news could show pictures of bloodied people coming out of the bombed Oklahoma City Federal Building. Television had a way of showing viewers the worst of the world. It could activate an audience by showing them what they should oppose. Television is at its best (or worst depending on your perspective) when the audience exclaimed, "That's terrible, I didn't know it was that bad!"

The power of negative news grew out of the civil rights demonstrations, campus protests, women's rights marches, and the end the war rallies. Until that time, viewers had been satisfied with Walter Cronkite, who carefully gave both sides of the conflict, but cable news quickly demonstrated that viewers wanted more entertainment with their news. Fox News built an audience of their own by telling people that the government doesn't work anymore; they also had a steady message, "It's really bad out there, and it's getting worse." Fear and anger continued to drive conservative cable news by grabbing public attention and telling their viewers that they should not trust the government. Added to this was the invention of Facebook that gave us more reasons to be angry and afraid.

Negative messaging not only increased interest, it divided people up into interest groups. Viewers became motivated by a single issue that was especially upsetting. It may have been hundreds of Hispanic children in cages along the Texas border – demonstrators out in front of a women's clinic that does late-term abortions – or teenage survivors of a school shooting that wanted to ban the sale of assault rifles. Single-issue politics was addictive. It divided people into smaller groups that would see the world through a single perspective. When television hammered on one political position there was no incentive to compromise with others. There was a stronger tendency to separate into factions that saw the world as being black and white.

Single-issue thinking has combined with uncompromising media tactics to shape a new form of toxic politics. We are moving closer to zero-sum politics whereby if I'm going to win, you're going to lose. The old method of sharing a victory is no more. In earlier times a member of Congress went back home and said, "We worked together with the other party and got some things done this year that I'm really proud about our cooperation." But in the present political climate it is more likely that the congressional member goes back home and says, "They were trying to get away with passing socialist legislation and I stopped them."

Governing is impossible if the main goal is negation. As a people we are focused on what we oppose, not what we favor.

NINE

Is Empathy a Burden?

W hy do liberals want to help folks who can't help them-selves? Why do left-wing folks see themselves as the self-appointed guardians of the least fortunate? Why are progressives willing to raise their own taxes for the benefit of people they don't even know?

Not long ago I organized a simulation game to be played with a group of men who were community leaders in Medford, Oregon. I had no idea that the game would reveal the basic differences that separate liberals and conservatives in meeting real-life problems. The game was designed to simulate the problems of poor people who wanted to improve their ghetto-like neighborhood by pooling their resources, getting involved in community action projects, and generally providing hope, despite the depressing circumstances of hardcore poverty. Each player drew cards that decided their individual fate. The different cards had an immediate impact on their life chances – they lost their jobs, their welfare payments were cut, they got evicted from their apartments, or they flunked out of school.

Included in the game was the enticing chance to engage in crime that might solve some of their short-term personal problems, but would cause the neighborhood to be infested with illegal drugs, an increase in street crime, with more of the players being arrested and sent to jail. It simulated bare-knuckled politics where everyone was on their own in a dangerous environment.

As the game progressed, players began to see that the odds were stacked against improving the neighborhood, and individuals turned to anti-social behavior as a means of survival. The simulated society became more dangerous as crime rates rose and individual players lost control of their future. Frustration turned to anger as players were pitted against each other for the scarce resources. Community action projects were abandoned because it simply made no sense to work together for long-term community improvement. Players felt increasingly isolated as the simulation degenerated into a crime-ridden situation that went steadily downhill.

There were eight people playing the game, but two of them stood out. First was the town mayor (a moderate Republican) who owned a successful local timber-products company. He was a solid conservative political leader who was the first to catch on to how to succeed while living in extreme poverty. It wasn't long before the mayor rose to become a crime boss by threatening low level criminals. At the end of the simulation, he was skimming ten percent off of all the illegal drug sales. He bought off the police and generally adjusted very well to the severe circumstances. The second person of interest was the editor of the local newspaper (a moderate Democrat) known as a "crusading liberal." In real life he supported local schools, defended civil liberties, community health clinics, and campaigned for measures to increase cooperation between the city and the county. But the editor had a problem: he couldn't bring himself in the simulation to engage in criminal behavior. He continued to sponsor community projects that failed miserably because other players would not support programs that didn't help them in the short run.

Everyone else in the simulation (the other seven players) adjusted to a life of crime in the game despite the fact that all of them (in real life) were law-abiding, upstanding members of their real community. In addition to the mayor and newspaper editor, there was one physician, an attorney, and four business leaders. In real life, none of them had ever engaged in crime.

After the simulation ended, we had a debriefing session to discuss the dynamics of the game. Seven of the eight players (excluding the editor) spoke of how they had to change and adapt to new circumstances as their lives were impacted by "terrible conditions" in the ghetto. The mayor was quite proud of himself as he spoke of how the "situation out on the street" evolved and how he applied "pragmatic strategies" to survive. The seven of them agreed that they learned something about how frustration could cause a person to break the law.

But the editor of the newspaper was very quiet. He sat over in a corner, chain-smoking. He was obviously frustrated by the simulation. Finally, the editor spoke up and said he had taken a "moral stand" in the simulation to help everyone else even though no one would work with him. He said he couldn't do the "wrong thing" even if it were only a game. It soon became clear that he personally couldn't let go of his "crusading spirit" because he said, it would have been "wrong."

The most intriguing part of the debriefing session was an unplanned, lengthy discussion about morality in politics, and how liberals wanted to lead the community to a "better place" even when many in the community didn't want to go. The editor confessed to being frustrated in his real life when individuals in his city voted against school levies and refused various reforms because it would raise taxes. He confessed that liberals were probably doomed to frustration because "doing the right thing" was often unpopular. In his words, people on the left have a "special burden" because they feel responsible for "everyone's welfare."

The mayor interrupted by saying, "I hope you don't mean to suggest that conservatives don't care. We do have a clear obligation to help people, but we believe that they should be responsible for their own lives," people need to be free to react to situations with pragmatic responses. He said everyone should feel responsible for their own lives, and no one should be a "self-appointed savior" for the community. The mayor added that – in real life – he never felt personally "devoted" to projects that involved everyone, and he couldn't understand why some people (like the editor) got so "hung up" on issues like improving city/country cooperation. The mayor laughed when he talked about the simulation. He added, "I could see that being a 'do-gooder' wasn't going to work so I did what I had to do."

Since that day, I've thought a lot about how the conservative mayor and the liberal editor acted, and how an allegory of the simulation could delve deeper into explaining how liberals and conservatives might see the morality of supporting programs that might be good for society, but unpopular with most of the voters. Perhaps the Affordable Care Act (Obamacare) was a prime example. Liberals enthusiastically put together a program that enabled about twenty million Americans to gain health insurance through a program that conservatives strongly opposed. What drove President Obama and the Democratic Party to launch a program that was to be so unpopular in the short run? Liberals were not set to profit from the program economically or even politically. They lost their congressional majority in 2010 and never recovered during Obama's remaining term of office. Leaders on the left knew they were taking a huge political gamble by pushing through a program that proved to be a huge political problem. So why did they do it?

And perhaps just as importantly, what motivated the Freedom Caucus of the Republican Party to fight Obamacare? They were also driven also by doing the right thing for the right reason – also with a sense of morality. As a matter of principle, these conservative Republicans could not vote for a government program that took away the freedom of individuals to provide for their own health care. They objected strongly to the idea that "health care was a right." GOP leaders contended that just because health care was important – didn't mean the government should make health insurance mandatory. They also stood firm on a moral political principle.

Liberals were motivated by a sense of empathy for people who couldn't afford health care. Progressives at all levels told stories about how ordinary, responsible folks filed for bankruptcies because they couldn't pay their medical bills. The liberal sense of empathy went into overdrive. You may remember the dedicated look in Obama's eyes as he defended Obamacare. He seemed to be motivated by something that he believed in, but something that brought him many sleepless nights. Obama, like the newspaper editor, was thinking about those lower-income folks who would benefit, but both Obama and the editor faced the public reaction from ordinary people who were saying: "I'd rather do it myself."

But health care is just the tip of the iceberg. The empathy/morality issue comes up in nearly every social welfare/civil rights issue on the books. Think outlawing racial discrimination, funding ghetto schools, voter suppression, women's rights, gerrymandering, community welfare centers, Medicare, Medicaid, Social Security, Head Start, food stamps, abortion, affirmative action, same-sex marriage, and most anti-poverty programs. The issue of left-wing morality comes into play on every program.

Liberals (like the newspaper editor) are committed to these kinds of programs even while they are criticized for waste, mismanagement, and questionable goals. People on the left often appear to be inflexible when they are not willing to abandon their original purpose of aiding the least fortunate. Conservatives, on the other hand, are more flexible (like the mayor) and are more pragmatic as they adjust to the reality of a situation.

The left is caught in the role of advancing humanistic goals, while the right enjoys the role of appearing to be more sensible and practical. Both stand by their moral principles. Maybe the editor was right – maybe empathy is a burden. What do you think?

Public morality is not something that can be proven; it's an abstract concept in the individual's conscience that motivates them to do the right thing for the right reason. The liberal sense of empathy is difficult to explain, but it comes up every time people on the left talk about the folks that are having trouble making ends meet. For progressives it is all about putting themselves in the shoes of those who have the least. Programs like these have only limited success, but liberals are willing to risk it all and accept that situation because they have a different moral mission.

But conservatives have a sense of public morality too. From their perspective it is immoral to undermine the human spirit by turning people into "wards of the state." They argue that everyone has to meet the challenges in life like getting sick, losing their jobs, or not saving enough to retire, and that individuals will learn a more important lesson in life if they have to take personal responsibility for their own welfare. There is an implication that the lessons of life should leave a scar that hurts a little – that the best way to learn is through the school of hard knocks. The traditional point of view is that government does not make people better by giving them things they do not deserve. Conservatives focus on the waste of a poorly designed, expensive program that never should have been enacted.

People on the right usually save the word "morality" for discussing religious or ethical concepts – of serving as an example to children, or behaving in an honest way that strengthens the family, and the country. Conservatives contend that they are not just cutting the funding of programs for their own self-interest. They believe that people have the potential to take care of themselves, and government should not stand in the way of folks becoming more independent.

Neither the left nor right is inherently wrong, but they certainly have a different vision of morality. Most conservatives and liberals don't understand each other. Folks on the right tend to get angry when they see a program they see as unnecessary or ill-conceived, while people on the left are dismayed when they hear critics say that everyone is on their own.

Both are like ships in the night they pass each other in the dark without appreciating how and why the other side applies a different set of moral standards to govern the nation.

TEN

Hanging Out with the Hells Angels

When we think of motorcycle gangs we don't ordinarily think about politics. The whole idea of burley gang members on their choppers brings up thoughts of strong-arm tactics and illegal operations, but not taking a political position. While this image may be accurate, there is often an ideological foundation that goes along with bikers who often have criminal records. I was to find out there's another side of the gang culture that is seldom noted.

One day I had lunch with an old friend in the San Francisco Bay area who had a pipe fabrication business. He had employed Ralph "Sonny" Barger, who was the leader of Hells Angels of Oakland. He said Sonny was a good worker, but he was arrested fairly often because of his criminal activities. The employer told him that the next time he missed work, he would have to let him go. It wasn't long before Sonny was arrested again and my friend fired Sonny Barger, but the two of them remained on good terms. I expressed an interest in meeting Sonny and the employer gave me his telephone number in Oakland.

Sonny Barger was the undisputed leader of the most famous Hells Angels motorcycle gang in the country. His name came up often involving drug busts and other illegal activities, but we almost never think about their sense of patriotism and pro-government values.

Behind his image as a fearless leader, Barger had a reputation for right-wing attitudes. He was a strong supporter of the Vietnam War. He actually had volunteered himself as the leader who would take a large group of Hells Angels to Vietnam to fight the Viet Cong and support US military forces in Vietnam. The expectation was that his gang would terrorize the Viet Cong. Can you imagine Hells Angels crashing through the jungle on their bikes chasing the Viet Cong? Apparently, Lyndon Johnson couldn't imagine it either.

Barger publicized the letter he sent to Johnson in 1965, but the President did not answer. Sonny repeated the story and referred to the "patriotism" of Hells Angels. Several times they volunteered to help police keep order at demonstrations in the Bay Area, but it usually meant the Angels would attack left-wing protestors. In several cases the violence actually began when the motorcycle gang got involved. The Oakland and Berkeley police kept telling the Angels they didn't need their help, but surprisingly, the Angels saw themselves as a group that favored keeping public order.

Just a few months before my arrival, the Oakland chapter of Hells Angels had served as a security detail at the Altamont Rock Festival. Sonny Barger and his Angels had been hired to keep order with the promise that they would get $500 worth of free beer. The end result was horrific. One of the drunken Angels stabbed a man, Meredith Hunter, who died from his wounds. There were fights on the festival stage and all over the grounds. There were three accidental deaths as well: two by a hit-and-run car accident, and one by an LSD-induced drowning in an irrigation canal. There had been a hope that Altamont would be remembered as "Woodstock West" (a place of peace and love), but it is remembered as a terrible disaster of uncontrolled violence with Hells Angels taking most of the blame.

My phone call to Sonny was rather brief. When I told him that I was a college professor from Oregon studying political unrest, he invited me over to the headquarters in a very nice Oakland neighborhood. There was a tall, chain-linked fence around the entire compound.

Two very large, barking, Doberman Pinscher dogs greeted me at the gate of the chain-link fence that surrounded the compound. I found out later that the attractive woman who let me in had been "Miss Oakland" the previous year. I was taken aback by the apparent wealth of Hells Angels. They had a mansion set back from the street on beautiful grounds. I expected they must be doing pretty well in all their illegal enterprises.

I had no idea of what to expect entering the inner sanctum of a motorcycle gang. Actually, it was quite elegant. There was a baby-grand piano in the middle of the great room and a two-foot metal sculpture of a monkey riding a Harley-Davidson sitting on top of a large black, polished table. There were hundreds of books on the floor-to-ceiling book shelves. The only thing that detracted from the classy atmosphere were the empty beer cans on the floor.

The most imposing thing about the room were eight members of the Hells Angels drinking beer and looking at me. Sonny introduced them all. The one I remember was "Animal" – who looked the part. He was a huge man with the look that he could do things to a person that would be messy. As I recall he had one eye that moved around the eye socket for no apparent reason. He and the others all appeared to be "battle tested" members of an outlaw motorcycle gang.

Soon after we sat down, Sonny drew my attention to the two Dobermans who were now sleeping on the floor. He said, "Watch my security system," as he opened the front door and yelled, "Kill mother-fucker." The dogs ran through the front door looking for someone to attack. It made everyone laugh – except me. It was obviously done to show me that my welfare was in their hands.

We spent the next hour sitting and talking in the main room. Everyone drank a lot of beer and took colored pills out of a large glass bowl. I had one beer and none of the pills I was offered.

It was during the summer of 1970, and out of nowhere, Sonny came up with the issue of the American Indians who had seized Alcatraz Island in San Francisco Bay. I don't know why it surprised me, but they all joined in condemning the Indians who they said were occupying a government-owned island. One guy said he wished he and the "Angels" could go out there and chase all of them off the "Rock," as he called it. I sort of thought the Angels might identify with the Indians who were also "law-breakers," but Sonny declared that he was a "taxpayer," and it made him "damn mad" that they had taken over government property. Then the conversation shifted to the Vietnam War protestors who were out on the street. Again, they sided with the government against the dissenters and told me of several times they had supported the police out on the street. Sonny proclaimed, "We have to beat them in Vietnam or they'll come to California."

Then out of nowhere Sonny said, "Would you like to go for a run?" In a few minutes we were outside as everyone started their bikes. Sonny motioned for me to get on his bike with him. There were eight bikes in all, going single file down a street. When we hit the freeway, everyone drove in pairs in the fast lane. I was too busy hanging on to notice very much, but I do remember the noise of the bikes caused all the other traffic to move over to the right. There was no question about who owned the road. It was a short ride and we went back to the house for some more beer and some of those colored pills in the glass bowl.

We all went into a shop-like room where some of the bikes were parked. I felt a little more confident as I asked Sonny, "If you side with the government on so many things, why are the police after you?" Sonny didn't answer the question but he rolled his eyes back and said, "If I would have been around one hundred years ago I would have had a gang that rode horses and robbed stage coaches." He then went on to lecture me on "gang politics" whereby he professed loyalty to the government as long as the Angels were free to do as they pleased. It occurred to me that the Angels are the ultimate example of "rugged individualists." They didn't care about anyone except themselves.

Sonny went on to say that most everyone he knew – in and out of prison – was pro-government, and that he still gets a "special feeling" when he sees the American flag. Another Angel added that their freedom is based on being able to ride their bikes any-where they pleased. No one mentioned the drug arrests or violent record the Angeles had.

I asked Sonny what he thought of the recent book Hunter Thompson had written about the Hells Angels. At the end of the book, Thompson described in great detail the thrashing he had received because he criticized one of the Angels for beating up his wife. Thompson said he feared he was going to be killed until Sonny stepped in and stopped the "pounding" he was getting from several gang members. Sonny made reference to the beating and said he didn't like Thompson's book. With a reflective look in his eye, Sonny said, "We should have killed the son-of-a-bitch."

As the day and evening wore on, there was always another can of beer being offered. I had not eaten since earlier in the day. It was clear that I was out of my league with these guys who seem to live on beer and those colored pills in a big glass bowl. After a couple more cans of beer, I made the mistake of saying that they had told me so much about themselves without knowing anything about me. It was a dumb thing to say. I've never have been a big beer drinker.

They took it the wrong way. The guy they called "Animal" dropped the wrench he had in his hand. I can still remember the sound of the wrench hitting the concrete floor. He narrowed his eyes and said, "Listen mother-fucker, if you were a cop, you'd be dead by now." I decided it was time to leave.

Driving back to Oregon, I thought more about the political attitudes and behavior of the outlaw motorcycle gang. They were right-wingers in the same way a lot of other folks were that didn't ride motorcycles. They reminded me of some folks with the similar view that "if they let me do my thing, I will be loyal," at least to the symbol of the government. Doing "my thing" might include peddling illegal drugs, or storming the US Capitol on January 6, 2021.

There is an unusual relationship between the violent right-wing fringe and their loyalty to the American principles they swear to defend. It is a complicated association in which they pledge allegiance to the government while they work to undermine that same government whenever it suits their needs. Somehow, they can love and hate the same set of institutions. Far-right militias of all varieties see no contradiction in being super patriots who are devoted to their government while using violence tactics against that government.

It is ironic that many of the AR-15 rifles bought today are purchased by "patriotic Americans" who pledge that someday they may take up arms against the government they profess to love. Many of them are preparing for the day when they may have to fight the US Army. If that day comes, the flag will be flown on both sides.

Those who stormed the Capitol on January 6th have a lot in common with Hells Angels. They just wear different uniforms.

ELEVEN

The Rotary Club Trap

Almost by accident I found two people in my political science course that had been pitted against each other in repeated violent confrontations out on the street before they moved to Oregon. They had been on opposing sides of protest demonstrations in northern California, especially in Berkeley. These two students actually remembered particular incidents when they were fighting for their lives. It was a frightening experience for both of them.

One student had been a member of the California Highway Patrol (CHP). He had retired early because of an auto accident while on duty, but he spoke to the class at length about the trying times he had breaking up protest demonstrations. As fate would have it, another member of the class had been a member of a radical group that had protested in some of those same demonstrations. The two shared details and discovered that they had been involved on opposite sides in the same riots on the UC Berkeley campus.

They spent a considerable of time reviewing dates and places. They both had remarkable memories and recalled specific events when the riots got completely out of hand. It was an emotional experience as they recounted times when they retreated in fear of being overrun.

The rest of us in the class watched and listened to them move from being enemies to becoming friends. It was an emotional process as they admitted the excesses on their own side during the riot. The end product was seeing their anger turn into understanding. It was a great learning experience as they confessed to losing their tempers and resorting to physical violence. It was an emotional time for both of them. There wasn't a dry eye in our classroom. They became our heroes because they were living proof that individuals in conflict could rise above their anger and hostility in a neutral setting. All of us in the class were proud of them.

I told a business friend of mine about the reunion of my two students. He thought they would make a fine program for the Medford Rotary Club. I recall the conversation the three of us had as we drove us to the Rotary Club meeting at the Rogue Valley Country Club in Medford. All three of us were prepared to serve as an example of how people could learn to cooperate despite the current hostilities out on the streets. We expected a very positive response.

I introduced my two students to the Rotary Club meeting and provided the details of how they had been enemies on the street, but how they gained an important insight as result of the class. Both of them told their story well with an emphasis on learning where and when they clashed. They each reported that they had gained a great deal by understanding the motives of the other side and how otherwise good folks could be swept up in ideological conflicts. The three of us thought we had done very well.

I remember feeling very confident as I took the floor to ask if there were any questions. The first question was really an accusation that the former CHP officer should have stayed in the service rather than going to college. They wondered if he no longer supported law enforcement groups who were trying to break up demonstrations. Next came the observation that the other student (who still had long hair) didn't sound very contrite in his comments. A Rotarian also asked if he supported the police or whether he might still go back out on the street. Then finally a question came for me from the local FBI agent who accused me of using a textbook written by a man who was a suspected Communist. At that point the entire audience of Rotarians seemed like they were ready to run us out of town. I thanked them quickly for the invitation and we fled the country club.

On the way back to campus the three of us discussed our utter failure in presenting what we thought was a favorable example of people gaining a precious insight through a common understanding. At that point we realized that the rotary folks didn't want to hear about reaching across the divide; they wanted to hear that law and order prevailed and that both students should agree to support the authorities. The Rotary Club crowd weren't ready to hear about how both sides could understand each other. They came down hard on all of us.

A few days later the three of us reported on our excursion to the class. Our experience stimulated an excellent discussion about the right and left in American politics, and how it was nearly impossible to please local conservatives with talk of accommodation and compromise. We also discussed why the three of us were so surprised by the Rotary response. We all agreed that we and the Rotarians were both stuck in our own respective worlds of expectations.

The Rotary Club members couldn't appreciate the fact that two students could form a friendship despite their opposing orientation, and we could not accept their rejection of our efforts. It was a great learning experience that set us back a few political notches in terms of thinking we could build bridges between contending groups.

Looking back, I can see how our naivety was a problem when we faced the Rotary Club. The three of us were so overconfident. We actually expected them to congratulate us for our putting aside the violent past and making amends.We had no idea that they would attack us. We were completely unprepared to defend ourselves. The attack caused us to feel immediate anger. It would have been so easy to strike back and accuse the Rotarians of being closed-minded bigots. Maybe they were, but it certainly wouldn't have been a good move to attack them in return.

Here is a case of how a surprise can blow up a situation that was expected to be smooth and noncontroversial. We didn't realize that there are folks out there who don't want to hear about any progress in reaching out across the divide. The Rotarians wanted to hear how the law came down hard on anyone who would cause disorder. They were expecting to hear that the left-wing radicals were defeated. The end result of our visit to the Rotary Club was that it caused their tempers to flare even more and turn them against the three of us who were trying to build a bridge between contending groups. We were all blind-sided by the entire process.

But our class learned something from our experience that was worth our humiliation at the Rotary Club meeting. It was that American conservatives are inclined to see protest demonstrations as battles that must be won by the police. They generally believe that protestors are wrong to begin with, so there is no need to meet them half-way or attempt to make peace with them. On the other hand, our class was influenced by liberal-type values that focused on finding a middle ground with the opposition. We were so idealistic in our thoughts.

The Rotarians had no interest in finding a common ground because they rejected the whole idea of people protesting against government policy. Next time we'll be more careful where we go to seek approval.

TWELVE

Meeting the Enemy

A friend of mine who was a psychiatrist spoke to my course on political extremism. He began his remarks by saying, "I've practiced psychiatry for thirty-seven years and I've never noted a characteristic in one of my patients I haven't already noted in myself – it's just a matter of degree." That fit my views about politics in the 1960s. It was "just a matter of degree" from the far left to the far right and everything in between.

I've always felt that there is no sharp break between conservatives and liberals, but there is an incremental change in the shading that occurs when moving from the left to the right. With this in mind I admonished my students to study themselves along with other people. The expectation was that they could develop some empathy for extremist groups on both ends of the political spectrum by trying to put ourselves in their place. It was "just a matter of degree." My thinking is that it's more difficult to hate someone if there is a feeling that everyone shares some part of our basic values.

My classroom was a meeting place for both sides. I invited armed White segregationists from the extreme right, Black revolutionaries from the left, and pretty much everyone in between.

On several occasions I literally had to tell my guests to leave their guns in their cars. None of the visitors got a chance to lecture the class. It was always an interview that I conducted with the guest. Everyone in class could ask questions. The only requirement was that the inquiries should be designed to let the guest lay out their essential beliefs. It was a basically a welcoming atmosphere in which the full ideological dogma could be advanced without much resistance. I suggested that students ask questions in a tone like "tell us more about how you feel about…"The goal for my students was to learn, not to win an argument. The end result was that students could actually understand why individual guests in the class became political activists. I think the visitors in the class felt that they had been given a fair hearing. Everyone learned something in the process.

I had a retired military officer in my class who was very far to the right. He could always be counted upon to voice strong opposition to everyone from the left. I recall the evening when I announced that a member of the Communist Party was going to be our guest at the next class meeting. First the officer questioned whether I had the right to bring a "Marxist" into a college classroom. Then he went on reciting all the conflicts around the world that had been inspired by various Communist organizations. He said that the Russian and Chinese had executed millions of people who resisted their rule. "What good," he asked, "could possible come from inviting a Communist to our class?" He next appealed to my sense of patriotism – did I still believe in American democracy? It was sort of an aggressive and nasty exchange of comments.

The former military officer worked himself into a lather – the more he talked, the angrier he got. Finally, he said he was considering going to the local newspaper and tell them what kind of people were speaking on the campus. At the end of the class period, he said he was so offended that he was dropping the class. There seemed to be nothing anyone could say to keep him on board. There were no good-byes as he stormed out of the classroom. But to my surprise he showed up at the next class meeting with the statement that he had never heard a Communist speak, and that he was coming back to challenge our guest. The former US Army major settled down in the front row so he wouldn't miss a word.

The Communist Party member was a local woman who had grown up in New York City. Her parents were Russian Jews who raised her to believe that the average, working-class person could make this a better world. At the age of sixteen, she joined the Young Communist League, which was the youth arm of the party. She grew up with personal friends that were to become the leadership of the American Communist Party. Among her friends were party leaders Eugene Dennis who would later become general secretary of the party, longtime member Harry Bridges who was a controversial San Francisco longshoreman, and Gus Hall who was chairman of the national party committee. One of her best friends was Peggy Dennis, wife of Eugene Dennis, General Secretary of the Communist Party. Our guest had married another party member who had been the editor of *The Daily Worker* newspaper in San Francisco.

This woman was very much an activist. She showed up at every left-wing protest demonstration in northern California and southern Oregon. She fit right into the leftist Ashland community. She was a feminist who was active in the "Ban the Bomb" movement and opposed the Pentagon in general. (Think Barbra Streisand in *The Way We Were*.)

Her opening comments to the class centered on her "terrible

personal crisis" she had in 1968 when the Soviets used tanks and guns against dissenting party members in Czechoslovakia. She watched filmed accounts of young, idealistic Communists being killed by Soviet troops. Her response was that she couldn't get the image out of her mind. It violated her faith in the Revolution because violence was being used against fellow party members who favored peaceful public participation. At first, she thought the press reports were just a part of "American Anti-Soviet propaganda," but latter she decided that what she saw on television was true. She said it "violated her soul" to see her "Soviet comrades" turn against other revolutionaries. It was a personal crisis that changed her life.

In a very dramatic manner, she outlined her steps in resigning from the international Communist Party organization, but to continue her commitment as a committed Marxist. In her mind, the Soviet Union's actions in Czechoslovakia had betrayed the principles of Marxism. She declared, from now on she would be an "independent Communist."

In a videotaped interview of the class, she spoke about her faith in humanity, concern for the poor, and hopes for minority groups around the world. She believed firmly that the Communist Party workers' class struggle would ultimately bring forth a better world for everyone. It was a consistent Marxist view.

I asked her how it felt to believe in all those things while watching the Soviet tanks literally crush fellow-revolutionaries in Czechoslovakia. She swallowed hard as she turned her head toward me and said, "How do you think it feels to find out your mother's a whore?"

I watched the retired military officer as our guest bared her soul. She was completely unguarded in her defense of Marxism, but critical of the dictatorial Russian leaders. When she advocated that Marxism should be taught in the American colleges and universities, the retired military officer gulped hard. He listened closely as she recounted her own life and how much faith she had in an ideology that would make the world more inclusive. The retired major was spellbound as she defended the right of all ideas to be welcome in the college curriculum. His face was beet red, but I couldn't tell what he was thinking.

At the conclusion of class, the retired officer moved in closer to our guest. The two of them spoke together in hushed tones over in a corner as everyone else left the classroom. The only part I did hear was when he asked if she would like to go out for coffee. I didn't know what to think as the two of them left the building together.

Later I heard – from both of them separately – that they had sort of become friends. The military man told me that he had a new respect for people who were the "outcasts of society." He said he could see why she had become a Marxist. Her comments were somewhat different. She said it was a welcome relief to be with someone who wanted to know how and why she had joined the Communist Party. They actually were talking to each other.

I must admit I was completely surprised by this new friendship. This was the time when many in the Rogue Valley still regarded left-wing people as a danger to society. Honestly, I expected that bringing the two of them together might cause the retired officer to go to the media and complain about allowing Communists on campus. But there was no follow-up story in the newspapers.

In this particular case I learned a new lesson that sometimes an ideological wall can be breached if people have a chance to see each other as human beings rather than enemies. The result can cut through a lot of ideological hatred in short order. Clearly the military officer had something close to a hatred for Communists, but those strong feelings were neutralized when he met a real, live woman who cared about helping others. He actually listened to her and told her how he felt about Marxism. But he continued to ask the question about why Communist governments use violence in stamping out their opponents? They had quite a discussion.

On the other hand, I didn't expect our member of the Communist Party would ever befriend a former military officer. She was pretty doctrinaire about rejecting the entire US military. She probably had something close to hatred for the whole US establishment. As far as she was concerned, the American military never deserved her respect. With this as a backdrop, the two of them coming together to talk was almost a political miracle.

In politics, making friends across the divide has the effect of creating an exception to previously held beliefs. The retired officer said later, "I still see Communism as the greatest danger to the world, but I do understand why she feels so strongly." She, on the other hand, said, "I guess I have a better idea of how he picked up his anti-Communist views."

Neither changed their minds, but their personal contact provided an allowance for an individual difference to their ideology. It's sort of like saying, "I still don't like them, but so-in-so is someone I can talk to." In this world of polarization, that's a step in the right direction.

Thousands of others who never have a face-to-face meeting are stuck in a deep rut created by years of distrust and suspicion. The trench of hatred has grown deeper each year. Middle America is immobilized by ideological symbols that have been strengthened since Donald Trump came on the scene. They disagree about nearly everything and the gap is getting wider every day.

Later I reflected on my psychiatrist friend who said he had "never noted a characteristic in one of his patients" that he hadn't already noted in himself. "It was just a matter of degree." It may be an intellectual stretch to conclude that Communist ideology is "just a matter of degree," but it certainly makes sense to view politics on a sliding scale from left to right.

The account of the avowed Communist and the retired military officer was a case in point. In that one particular case they actually bridged the gap by listening to each other. It might help a bit if more folks got to know someone personally from the "other side."

THIRTEEN

Falling in Love –
Falling in Line

O ne of the most dramatic statements I've ever made in the
classroom was, "Democrats fall in love while Republicans
fall in line." It was my opening comment to begin the segment on
the kinds of people that are attracted to each of our political parties.
It's a catchy way to begin the topic, but my students wanted real-
life examples that are happening today.

I told them that Democratic liberals are very unruly – they love
knock-down-drag-out debates in public before they settle on a
policy or candidate. But when they do, their attachment is at an
emotional level. Democrats need to "fall in love" with their political
positions and candidates. Their loyalty can't be bought. They need
to be personally convinced. Folks left-of-center have to "feel" an
allegiance before they're willing to go out and commit themselves.

By comparison, Republicans and conservatives are more orderly
and seem more restrained in how they act in public. Folks in the
GOP are less committed to particular policy goals and they are
more likely to close ranks around issues while in the public spot-

light. They may disagree in private as they do with their right-wing fringe groups, but they seldom air their dirty linen in public. After a policy position is decided or a candidate is chosen, they usually "fall in line."

The American humorist Will Rogers once said, "I'm not a member of any organized political party. I'm a Democrat." Progressives actually love that quote because it describes their own free-for-all behavior. Bill Clinton said working with Democratic members of Congress was "like herding cats." Liberals are known more for their disagreements than for their discipline. They constantly question the motives of their opponents within their own political party, and they often divide into warring factions. They always seem to be disagreeing with their leaders and with each other. Democrats love to tell stories about how they view "principle above party."

In contrast, conservatives are more willing to swallow their differences and close ranks behind a single leader inside a more structured organization. Because of this tendency to "stay in line," GOP efforts are generally better organized, and more successful. Folks on the right are more likely to get things done in politics because they seldom disagree publicly and are more disciplined and more willing to stay on message.

The two parties actually view political power differently. Democrats are almost apologetic when they hold a large party majority in Congress. They seem uncertain about how to use that power to enact their agenda. Liberals sometimes worry about appearing to be too uncompromising in their stature. Republicans, however, are quick to use any and all power at their disposal. We seldom if ever see Republicans hesitate or voice a concern about appearing to be too partisan. They are eager to gain their objectives no matter how it may look on the outside. Winning is the main objective for conservatives; they know that most voters will forget the details before election day.

Democrats generally have a long list of what they intend to do if elected – winning elections for them is a means to an end. Republicans, on the other hand, seldom have a long list of objectives; winning is their objective. Other than tax cuts, voting restrictions and cutting government regulations, the GOP adjust their campaign to winning the most votes. Getting and using political power is their main goal.

Republicans are really good at following a leader, but what happens when the leader is Donald Trump? The short answer is they follow him anyway and remain silent in the short-term because they don't want to upset their base of voters who approve of Trump. Dissatisfied Republicans may feel unhappy about day-to-day affairs with Donald Trump, but they don't want to talk about it in public. GOP members of Congress are unusually quiet when Trump's behavior is being discussed.

This situation gets worse, though, when the public and private sides are far apart. In political campaigns, Republican Party members know what they favor, but they find themselves thoroughly frustrated by their own leader, Donald Trump, who often sprouts ideas that rank-in-file Republicans oppose. Somehow, they have to answer for "that man" who has behaved in a reckless manner and changed what their party stands for.

On the other side, Democrats are forever disagreeing and breaking into factions. President Joe Biden knew what would happen when the progressive wing and the moderate wing begin to quarrel. It was not uncommon for one or two Democrats to hold back the whole party; they mumble in public about they wished their leader had more courage. There doesn't seem to be anyone in their party who can crack the whip with progressive Democrats to get everyone in line.

Republicans don't quarrel and disagree about things in public. They usually line up on issues without a public debate. The only exception would be members of the Freedom Caucus and followers of right-wing fringe groups that are strong supporters of gun rights. The far-right members of Congress are the only exception of GOP members who don't fall in line.

Democrats are known for being attracted to idealistic causes, but they often don't have the stomach for a fight when the votes are stacked against them. For example, when Supreme Court Justice Anthony Scalia died unexpectedly in February of 2016, Democratic President Barack Obama was entitled to nominate a new justice to the Supreme Court. But to the surprise of nearly everyone, Republican Senator Majority Leader Mitch McConnell announced a "new rule" that, because it was an election year, they would not even consider an appointment until after the people had voted in November. Democrats thought they were going to win the White House in 2016 so they didn't offer much of a fight. But the boldness of the Mitch McConnell action paid off when Trump won and he appointed a conservative to the Supreme Court in 2017.

At times like this Democrats can be real wusses. They mumbled about the selection of a new Supreme Court judge "not being fair," but progressive Democrats didn't offer much real resistance. Unlike Republicans, Senate Democrats held back at a crucial time even when protocol was on their side. The GOP outmaneuvered them, plain and simple. Senate Democrats could have tried to rally the country behind their cause, but they chose not to go into battle. It's difficult to get the Democrats off their rear-ends unless they take up the cause of fighting against some injustice.

They are able to visualize how society can be improved, but they don't seem to have the stomach to fight in a clinch.

Democratic presidents often idealize their administrations with grand names: FDR had the New Deal; Truman had the Fair Deal; Kennedy had the New Frontier; and LBJ had the Great Society. Republicans, on the other hand, are less motivated about improving society; they frequently focus on how they will hold back the government or even disable it. In recent years, Republicans have focused on the charge that "government does not work," and when they win, they prove it.

Many citizens are uplifted by hearing about liberal programs that will help the least powerful achieve their goals. Conservatives don't feel the need to raise the public's expectations because they are more likely to repeal the programs that liberals have enacted.

Liberals secretly envy conservatives because people on the right of center are more effective in developing a united front for political combat, and they fight to win. Republicans learned long ago that using aggressive tactics works well in politics, especially when your party is more united than the opposition. Preparing to win elections for the sake of winning seems to motivate Republicans more than Democrats.

Democrats have been known to turn on their own leaders and criticize each other in public. There's a built-in division between progressive and moderate Democrats. There's always an intra-party battle going on. Senior Democratic leaders complain they spend a lot of time and energy just trying to keep peace in their political family, reassuring their voters to stay in the fold and stay "in love" with their own party. There are frequent efforts among progressives to promote side issues such as racial integration, women's issues and voting rights. Moderates are forever saying that these progressives are being "carried away" with policies that are too far left of the voting public.

GOP leaders and voters are much more cohesive. They complain less about issues that don't concern them directly. There's a loud silence among Republicans when questions of racial equality, or gender issues are discussed. As expected, conservatives usually "fall in line," as they are willing to overlook the pleas coming from low-income voters.

By comparison, many Democrats can't seem to overlook any of the burning equality issues of the day; they are like a moth to a flame as they seek out controversial positions that make them appear to be divided and too idealistic. Left-wing Democrats in Congress usually propose special amendments that aid the least fortunate members of society.

Progressives through the ages have often been swept up in a cause that they believed in for the sake of human rights. It has not been uncommon for people on the left to show their emotions about issues they feel are more important than themselves. Liberals see themselves as the self-appointed guardians of human rights They love to lock arms, march, and sing as they stand up for the least fortunate against the wealthy in the establishment. It is an old story of Blacks singing Gospel songs, women marching for equal rights, labor union members standing in a picket line, and farm workers fighting for a union contract. The left often turns out thousands of committed followers but they still lose the battle.

There's a kind of mystical feeling among progressives even when they lose. I recall talking with an old leftist revolutionary who went off to Spanish Civil War of 1935. With a straight face he said, "We had the best songs, but they had the most guns." In the end, the side with the most guns usually win. That's true in

American politics as well. Liberals often sing and shed tears when standing up for the human rights of the oppressed. It takes a lot more than that to make conservatives cry.

Across the country there are more Democrats than Republicans. Because of the numerical advantage, Democrats have a good chance of winning if they can register their people and get them out to vote on Election Day. When there is a heavy voter turnout it generally means Democrats will do well. Of course, Republicans know this, and that's why the GOP favors almost any means to suppress the vote, including voter ID laws, reducing the number of polling places, cutting back on voting by mail, and purging the voting rolls if people miss voting in a single election.

Even the weather plays a role in this partisan competition: rainy, cold weather usually mean more Republican victories because conservatives are more disciplined and motivated to vote. GOP voters are also more likely to have their own transportation and jobs where they can take off time to vote. By comparison, lower income folks and minority group members are less reliable as voters. They sometime need a bit more encouragement to leave work early or arrange for a ride to the polls. As a rule, Democrats do better when election days are warm and dry, when the sun is shining, and when there are exciting social issues on the ballot.

Some things never change: In the future, Democrats will continue to fall in love while Republicans will continue to fall in line.

FOURTEEN

What the Nazis
Did to Us

O ne of the most interesting times of my life was spent in Israel on a Fulbright scholarship. I was in Jerusalem most of the time, but I had free rein to travel around and talk to members of the Israeli government, cultural leaders, and university faculty members. I didn't realize at the time that some my experiences in Israel would follow me home and play out in an emotional, religious meeting in Medford, Oregon.

It had been many years since the Holocaust of WWII, yet I found the shadow of the tragedy still haunted the Jewish people who had survived one of the most barbaric periods of history. The topic was never far away from those who lived it. It has been said of the Holocaust that, "Not all the victims were Jews, but all the Jews were victims." The horrific experience of the Holocaust made an impact on Jews all over the world. They identified with the victims as they still do today.

I attended many lunch-time lectures at the Hebrew University in Jerusalem where a crowd would gather to hear and discuss a topic. The speaker on this particular day did not give his name, but he was apparently a well-known member of the academic community in Jerusalem. He was a sociologist who began his presentation by pulling up his sleeve and showing the numbers tattooed on his arm. He was a Holocaust survivor who had immigrated to Israel from Poland. He went on to say that he had spent his entire academic life on the subject of how the Israelis treated the Palestinians.

His opening point was that violent experiences in life shape individual behavior, stressing the fact that upward of 30 percent of children who are beaten severely by their parents grow up to be child-beaters when they become parents. He went into statistical and anecdotal evidence backing up his claim, noting how the memories of being beaten cause many to repeat that practice when they are placed in positions of authority. His examples included severe cases of "cycles of violence" when abused people vented their violence on others. His main argument was that the practice of using brutal force against people can actually become part of a culture.

Then he made the statement that angered nearly everyone in the room: "What the Nazis did to us, we are doing to the Palestinians." The reaction was immediate: one plastic lunch box was thrown, several cups and plates and a half-eaten orange landed near the speaker. From that point on the presentation was a free-for-all with shouts of denunciation in several different languages. I tried to approach the speaker, but he left the room quickly as people appeared ready to attack him. I listened to the comments from others milling around. They were all negative. I remembered an older woman saying over and over, "How could he say that?" Others questioned whether he really had been in the death camps. I didn't hear or see anyone who supported his assertions about the treatment of Palestinians. I wondered at the time if anyone there agreed with him, but I didn't feel comfortable asking anyone in that room. The event never left my mind, I can remember it like it was yesterday.

Months later, I returned to Oregon where I was interviewed by a reporter from the *Medford Mail Tribune.* The journalist was looking for an interesting insight into the current conflict in Israel. I recounted the story about the Israeli sociologist. The newspaper reporter handled it very carefully with quotation marks around the charge about the Nazis' influence. I had no idea that the story would be considered controversial.

But three days later I was visited in my home by two very nervous rabbis. I had never met either one of them, but I welcomed them into my home. After a few minutes they began the conversation by saying that they knew many people who said they had known me for more than twenty years, but didn't realize I was "anti-Semitic."

I was shocked by this charge. I couldn't imagine that repeating the story from the professor at the Hebrew University in Israel would make me anti-Semitic. I called attention to the quotation marks, but the rabbis were undeterred. They said just repeating such a story was proof that "I was anti-Semitic." At this point, I became angry and asked for a chance to come to the synagogue to explain the situation. The older rabbi said it was "out of the question," that I was not Jewish and therefore could not address the congregation. I insisted, saying I had a right to defend myself from those who thought I harbored prejudice.

I raised my voice, asking – then I demanded – that I had a right to tell my side of the story. Finally, the younger rabbi acknowledged that maybe there would be an interest in hearing about the incident from my point of view.

On the next Friday evening my wife and I went before a congregation of about eighty people in Medford. The men were on one side of the room and the women were all on the other side. I didn't detect any positive response from the men as I recounted the story. I noticed that they all sat there with their arms folded across their chests. On the women's side there were attentive looks that gave me the impression that they were there to listen, not to condemn.

Here I was a Gentile standing alone, speaking to a group of Jews about Israel and a very unpopular analysis set out by a Jewish sociologist who had survived the Holocaust. It was a completely unexpected situation whereby a group of American Jews in Medford, Oregon, was engaged in a debate on how the Israeli state treats Palestinians thousands of miles away in the Middle East.

That evening in Medford, my knowledge of Jewish history was sketchy at best, but I do remember saying that the Jewish people (because of their history) should be more sensitive than anyone about violence and discrimination. I tried to be objective and provide some understanding of why there was so much emotion on the subject. I could tell by the body language of the men in the room that I was not succeeding.

Several men in the back interrupted me with loud voices, making very negative statements about "Palestinian terrorism," and why it was necessary for the Israeli Defense Force (IDF) to use strong-arm tactics. That brought an equally strong response from several women in the front row on the other side of the room, charging that the IDF was betraying Jewish values. There were tears in the eyes of some women as they pleaded for a less aggressive approach on the West Bank.

A highly-spirited, unregulated debate ensued between several angry men in the back yelling at the women in the front. After a few minutes, no one seemed to pay much attention to me. Unknowingly, I had activated tempers on both sides of the controversy. After about ten minutes of a free-for-all, one of the rabbis thanked me for coming to the synagogue. Folks on both sides were shouting at each other as I left the room.

I realized once again that Jews all over the world have a personal interest in Israel and what happened during the Holocaust. One cannot visit Yad Vashem, the Holocaust Museum in Jerusalem, without coming away with images of utter cruelty and mass genocide that was visited on the defenseless European Jewish community. There are displays of the artifacts left behind by the children – their drawings, letters, diaries, and toys. Words cannot describe the account of how six million people were murdered because of their ethnic, religious heritage.

Perhaps the one unifying factor of the Jewish people today is that they all feel the heartbreaking history of the Nazi gas chambers as helpless victims were led to their deaths. "NEVER AGAIN" says it all. The echoes of that pledge are still being heard loud and clear, but the discrimination against the Jews continues. Anti-Semitic behavior is actually increasing around the world. There is a real fear among Jews every time an anti-Semitic event occurs.

The memory of the Holocaust illustrates that Israeli Jews have a split personality that represents both the powerless and the powerful. First there is the account of how six million Jews were herded into railroad cars, sent to the death camps and massacred without mercy. On the other hand, Israeli Jews today have one of the best-trained, best-equipped armed forces in the world. It is as though they are making certain that they will never again be led to their deaths as a powerless people.

Nearly everyone in Israel serves in the military and there are guns everywhere. In a sense, each Israeli is repeating the phrase "Never Again" as IDF soldiers go about their daily routine with an assault rifle slung over their shoulder. They don't seem to be boisterous about their weapons; it is more a matter of a resolute, personal necessity to survive in a nation surrounded by unfriendly neighbors. Yes, all Jews were "victims." And that status is always in their minds.

The situation in Israel today sets out a principle that should be noted: repression may bring forth obedience in the short run, but it builds a legacy of resentment that may last forever. The IDF certainly is one of the most effective fighting-force in the world, but it has not built the peace and security that the Israeli Jews seek.

Repression fosters terrorism, it does not eliminate it.

FIFTEEN

The Ku Klux Klan as Victims

S lavery was never practiced in Oregon, but it was known as a "Whites Only State" during most of the nineteenth century. In 1844, Black exclusion laws were enacted in the "Oregon Country." Later in 1865, Oregon was one of fifteen states that refused to ratify the 15th Amendment (giving Black men the right to vote). There were many prominent members of the Klan in recent Oregon history. Walter M. Pierce (D) of Pendleton was elected governor of Oregon in 1922, and Kaspar K. Kubli (R) of Jacksonville was elected Speaker of the Oregon House in 1923. They were both Klansmen and were well-known for their racist views. The Ku Klux Klan had an important political role in both political parties.

The Klan had large local organizations in Portland, Ashland, Medford, Eugene, Grants Pass, Salem, Astoria, Hood River, and Pendleton. Today, Portland is still known as the "whitest big city" in the US, and Oregon is approximately 86 percent White. Despite the progressive tradition in Oregon, there are still a lot of racial tensions throughout the state.

My interest in the Klan began reading press accounts in Oregon history, but I broadened it with a series of interviews I did several years later with current Klan members after mass rallies in Louisiana and Mississippi. At first, I had some apprehension about going to these rallies because of the violent reputation of the Klan, but I soon discovered that they were mostly ordinary, hometown people who were the product of their own environments.

When I attended the Klan meetings, I was working as a free-lance journalist which was perceived by Klansmen as a great opportunity for press coverage. My approach was strictly objective, asking open-ended questions so they could tell their story. I worked by myself with nothing but my press credentials, a ball-point pen, and a reporter's notebook. Everyone could hear my northerner accent. I also had Oregon auto license plates so there was always some suspicion of why I was there. I introduced myself as "Bill Meulemans," and I was surprised that they usually remembered my first name throughout our conversations.

Klan members were understandably cautious because there had been many attempts by law enforcement agents to infiltrate their ranks. For this reason, I never asked for any personal information and they, in turn, were careful not to give me any details about themselves. My questions were always general in nature. I always made it a practice to present myself honestly because I had nothing to hide. I learned early on in life, when doing interviews with folks on the extreme right and left, always tell the truth. If they catch you in a lie there could be real problems.

These Klan get-togethers were clearly a chance for the whole family to come out and talk about issues that concerned them all. There were an unusually large number of young men present. Some Klansmen had on the full regalia of gowns and hoods, but nearly all the people were just in street clothes. I didn't stand out as an outsider in the crowd, and contrary to my earlier feelings, I felt completely safe.

The four Klan rallies I attended were very similar, featuring a speaker from out of town who would excite the crowd with condemnations of the Black civil rights leaders, the so-called Jewish conspiracy, and the intrusive actions of the federal government. In each case there were burning crosses of various sizes that supplied an eerie glow to the whole gathering.

These public meetings were held during the early summer in the evening. All of them were outside in open fields at the edge of small towns. There were home-made signs posted noting the time and place of each gathering. I was always on the look-out for these signs along the road that directed me into small towns off the major highways.

My tactic was to ask questions to men standing near me about who was speaking tonight and what was going on locally. Typically, I would say something like, "Boy this is quite a turnout," before asking anything about the rally itself. The northern accent of an outsider always made heads turn. My introduction to them was I am writing for a newspaper in Oregon, which was true. I had press credentials, but no one ever asked to see them. Sometimes I asked about the local high school football team, which always got a quick response.

It's amazing how fast one can strike up a conversation with total strangers when a person is alone. People love to talk, especially about what makes them proud or angry. Their pride was in being White and their anger was about national political leaders. These two themes were woven into all the speeches at the Klan rallies. From their point of view, their local way of life was being threatened, and coming to the rally was one way they could express their fears about the present.

As each event was winding down, I would continue to talk to men in small groups at the meeting site, in parking lots, on park benches, and in one case, at a local tavern. There was always a thin line when I knew it was time to stop asking questions. Instinctively, I knew when I was pushing them too far. I was alone in their town. It was important not attract unwanted attention. Those who attended the rallies always turned the topic to race and the federal government trying to shove integration "down their throats." I took a lot of notes so the participants felt they were being heard.

The conversation focused on their hatred of Black civil rights leaders and their delight in the assassination of Martin Luther King just a few years before. My role was to ask questions and never argue. I was the uninformed northerner who obviously didn't know much about the South. The questions were all soft-ball inquires under the general heading of "how do you feel about that?" All my contacts were with young men in street clothes who took this an opportunity to tell their story.

Generally, the longer we talked the more comfortable was the conversation. Only on one occasion did I speak briefly to a Klansman who was dressed up in his robes. That was a very different experience. I soon discovered how intimidating it was to make eye contact with a person wearing a hood with eye-holes cut out. Seeing the dim outline of the eyes and hearing a deep voice coming from inside made me wonder if I was safe speaking to someone who advocated violence, or perhaps had engaged in some actions against specific victims. I had no specific reason to feel threatened, but the whole Klan regalia made my blood pressure go up a few points.

The man in his robes spoke with a little more authority than the others. He specially wanted to know more about me and why I was there. It was at that point that I realized that the Klan had a certain mystique designed to terrify an outsider like me. There was something about the hood that sent shivers down my spine. Afterwards I imagined what it must be like to be an African-American or a Jewish person to face this figure on a back street in a small town, and to remember that local law enforcement officials aren't known for protecting a stranger with a northern accent.

All the Klan members brought up the "defender role" as their purpose for being; usually it was protecting White women from Black men who they imagined were just waiting to rape "their women." The other theme was the need to halt the integration process in public schools. The stories were long on emotional anger and short on specifics. It reminded me of the kinds of stories one would hear in a high school boys' locker room that were embellished to make them more interesting. But there was a kind of a built-in excitement to be at a Klan meeting where everyone was eager to be jacked up by stories that were based more on fear than fact.

The issue of "race-mixing" came up at every rally. One speaker up on stage likened it to letting a "mongrel bull" getting loose with defenseless, "purebred cows." In small groups it was discussed as the most disgusting thing one could imagine. There was always a sexual connotation, and there was always a theme of defending of the "White race." The fear was the intentional weakening of the White race by mixing with "Jews" and "Niggers." It was described as a disgusting outcome that ordinary people wouldn't know about unless they came to a Klan meeting.

One night, after a rally, there were four young men (in street clothes) who sat outside with me on a park bench about thirty yards from the burning cross that cast a bright glow over the departing crowd. One of the younger men said he felt like the Civil Rights Movement was "threatening his way of life" and that he had to "fight back." Another said Black people were getting financial help from "New York Jews." The four men displayed their own uncertainties saying that they were really on their own with no "outside help."

It seemed a great irony that these working-class men, who liked to talk about terrorizing Black people, had cast themselves in the role of a minority. They appeared to feel unsure about themselves and the future of the Klan. But the burning cross, just a short distance away, must have given them a sense of self-importance in being involved in a cause that was bigger than life.

In another group, one man asked if I would try to reach northerners to tell them about the dangers of the Civil Rights Movement. He said the Klan was just trying to "save America." He feared what he called, "the mongrelization of America," where the White race would cease to exist because of inter-racial sex. When this man spoke of "defending our women," everyone else nodded their heads. There was the continuous theme of "standing up for America" and defending the "weaker sex." They saw themselves in a lonely struggle with no support coming from the rest of the country.

In each of these conversations I brought up the question of why Klan members felt so strongly about opposing integration. They had an eager response: first came the denial that they "hated" anyone even though I had not used the word. Next there was a condemnation of the media that they said focused on the few cases where violence had occurred.

But the main message always turned on how they are being

forced to go to school with "Niggers." The source of that problem was always discussed in absolute terms with no gray areas. It was Washington, D.C., the "hotbed" of enemies in the Congress, the White House and the Supreme Court – all sympathetic to "Kikes, Niggers and Papists." They assured me that the Klan was the only group that they could depend on.

As the evening progressed, they relished telling personal stories about how their "daddies" had raised them to defend the White race and stand up for America. Then they asked me the question, "Wouldn't you stand up for your family?" Of course, I had to nod and agree. There was an ever-present sense among them that history was a series of one-sided actions against "the White man." The aftermath of "The War Between the States" was brought up as an example of how the rest of the country was insensitive to their needs as a people.

Several times they spoke of how Christians in the South had been a friend to "Negroes," and how secure and orderly life had been for Black people before the Civil Rights Movement. The message was that northerners were badly "misinformed" about history. Newspapers like the New York Times and Washington Post were the main culprits.

No one mentioned "slavery" or the "Jim Crow" era, but it was lurking in every conversation as they discussed how it "used to be." Phrases like, we all got along "really well" was a code for defending the Old South. I could sense that integration was a psychological enemy for these unskilled White men who were near the bottom of the social structure. It must have been satisfying for members of the Klan to have someone beneath them.

Most of the time I felt completely safe, but there was one night that was more threatening. The particular night I ended up in a local tavern. It felt different from all the other evenings. That night everyone had several beers as we sat at a table over in the corner near the shuffleboard. I had one beer all night long. After two hours or so, the increasing number of beers seemed to make everyone a bit more confrontational. They spoke of "Niggers," and what they would do to get one alone on a dark street. In their excitement, they leaned forward and involuntarily spit in my face.

At this point I stopped asking questions – they were interrupting each other in a continuous lecture about what the Klan would do to local Black people they mentioned by name. The language got stronger and stronger. Taking notes was not appropriate. I just sat back and listened.

As the night wore on, individual members said they had to go home because tomorrow was a work day. Finally, there was just one man left with me at the table. The bartender said he wanted to close so we walked outside. At this point a small house cat walked up to us on the sidewalk and rubbed against the other man's leg. While continuing to talk (he looked me straight in the eye) and reached down and picked up the cat and rung its neck then dropped the dead cat on the sidewalk.

I was horrified, saying, "Why the hell did you do that?" His response, "It was only a cat." I asked again, and this time he seemed a bit put-off by my anger. Suddenly, I realized the ease with which he killed the cat and I was struck by fear for my own safety. Never before have I seen such a cold, uncaring look in someone's eyes while killing a defenseless animal. It almost seemed like a warning to me. Suddenly I felt I was in the company of a person who could kill easily with no personal feelings. He had a blank expression on his face. I was clear that his killing the cat didn't matter to him.

But it did matter to me. I had an immediate response as I shouted, "That's it," as I walked away in disgust.

The last thing I heard him say was, "But it was only a cat." I drove to the next town looking for a motel. For some reason I didn't feel safe anymore in that community. That was my last Klan meeting. I remember that part of the evening especially.

My experiences with the Klan reenforced a couple of thoughts. First, there are still a lot of right-wing militia groups that believe they are trying to "save America" through violent acts. Until recently their biggest problem was that so few people would follow them. But the difficulty in recruitment doesn't seem to be such a problem now. And secondly, there's now a ready-made White supremacy constituency for a leader like Donald Trump outside of the South. The storming of the Capitol on January 6th illustrated that the potential for violence is not limited to one section of the country. It's pretty clear that right-wing militia groups have benefited directly from Donald Trump's public antics. His negative comments about Blacks, Latinos and Muslims have played well among White, working-class men who fear they are becoming a smaller minority in America.

Klan members and others say they admire Trump because he "Stands up for America." Where this will lead, no one knows for sure.

SIXTEEN

Surrounded by Threats

Throughout history the American people have spent a lot of time creating a defense against threats both inside and outside their country. Some of our most dramatic moments have occurred when we felt threatened by some malevolent force. The increasing levels of real or imagined fear today is one of the reasons why we are so divided as a people.

The current situation in the United States is even more complicated by the fact that an ever-increasing number of Americans feel threatened by each other. Additional reasons to be afraid come daily from Facebook and cable-news outlets. Thousands – perhaps millions – are fearful about their futures, and it's getting worse. Folks on both sides of the spectrum feel threatened.

Many Oregonians feel fortunate that they live in a state where folks seem to get along pretty well. It may surprise them to discover there are twenty identifiable groups there that feel threatened by their fellow citizens.

- Blacks have a fear of aggressive police treatment and the prospect of being killed.

• Whites feel threatened by a growing number of non-whites and people of other cultures.

• Muslims face continued marginalization by a large segment of the American public.

• Hispanics live in fear of deportation and wide-spread public discrimination.

• Homeless people, labeled as nonpersons, fear they will be removed from society.

• Women are threatened by sexual abuse, mistreatment and economic discrimination.

• LBGTQ+ folks feel vulnerable in a political system that may strip them of their rights.

• Moderates are alarmed by the rise of militias and others that undermine the rule of law.

• First Amendment supporters have a growing fear that the free press is being minimized.

• Workers feel threatened by the growth of automation that is taking away their jobs.

• Gun owners are fighting government restrictions on buying and carrying of firearms.

• Evangelical church groups feel threatened by anti-religious policies and secularism.

• Children have a daily fear that they may be targeted in mass school shootings.

• Environmentalists are worried about the dangers of pollution and climate change.

• College students are angry about rising tuition costs and fewer career opportunities.

• Young wage-earners have a real fear that the Social Security System will go broke.

• Elderly people feel powerless about rising crime rates and increased living costs.

• Defenders of democracy are worried that there will be another armed insurrection.

• Veterans are discouraged by the marginal treatment of injured military service personnel.

• Covid-19 has threatened everyone and there is fear that the vaccine may not defend us.

When people feel threatened and fearful, they become anxious and combative. Each group is pitted against others. There is widespread fear that their particular group is "losing ground." Many feel the need to use stronger tactics against their opponents. The present situation is bringing out all the worst features of tribalism. It has developed into zero-sum thinking – the fear that if someone else wins "we" will automatically lose. This is the kind of political environment that has paved the way for an authoritarian leader to come on the scene.

Added to this is the feeling that many people are locked into competing sides. They are Democrats vs. Republicans – liberals vs. conservatives – White vs. Black – Hispanic vs. Anglo – rural vs. urban – rich vs. poor – male vs. female – gay vs. straight – Wall Street vs. Main Street – young vs. old – union vs. non-union – religious vs. secular, and a whole host of other divisions that relate to Covid-19, guns, cultural issues, income inequality, health care, climate change, gender roles, abortions, taxes, immigration, and the environment. It's a tough world out there and everyone feels they have to be on guard!

Identity politics goes hand in hand with fears and threats, and cable news shows stoke the fires on a daily basis. Misinformation and downright lies are broadcast daily to make folks feel more afraid. It isn't long before they start blaming folks down the street. Does this sound familiar?

There are many examples of this conflict in Oregon, especially in the Portland Metro area. The Proud Boys have a persistent feeling that they are under attack and that they need to fight back. The left-wing response is headed up by ANTIFA who are proud to be anti-racist and anti-fascist. Their motto says it all: "Sometimes Antisocial – Always Antifascist." Both groups have been involved in a nearly endless number of demonstrations and incidents.

Rioting has been on the increase in Portland since the election of Donald Trump. Hundreds have been arrested and property damage has been extensive. Gang violence and random shootings have also increased sharply. There is a fear on all sides that the other side is winning. In the meantime, most citizens of Portland feel they are surrounded by an "outside threat" they can actually see and feel. For them, Portland is no longer what it used to be. Folks are afraid to go downtown. Many think the city will never be a place where people feel safe.

Now, what can we do about it?

SEVENTEEN

Souls That Can Be Saved

O ne day I received a telephone call in my office from a woman named Rita who said she and other parents in her community needed political help. She lived in the Phoenix-Talent School District located between Ashland and Medford. Rita's concern was that the school district had not been able to pass school levies for several years. She was a parent of three children, and her fear was that the quality of their educations had suffered because the District didn't have the funds to maintain a high quality education. According to Rita, the District had a favorable response in most of the voting precincts except those with a high percentage of retired people. "The real problem," she said, "was the Rogue Valley Manor. They're in our school district and they have a lot of people up there on the hill who turn out to vote against funding our schools."

Anyone who has spent much time in the Medford-Ashland area knows about the Rogue Valley Manor. It is a large building perched up on a hill with many windows looking down on Interstate 5 between Medford and Ashland. The ten-story Rogue Valley Manor is the tallest building in the Rogue Valley. It is an up-scale retirement home that draws in upper-income seniors who want a spectacular view of the entire Rogue River Valley.

According to Rita, retired people in the Manor took every opportunity to vote against raising taxes for the local schools. She wondered if anyone in the Political Science Department could help pass the school levy coming up next year.

As fate would have it, I was offering my Political Campaigning course during the coming Fall Quarter. I invited Rita and several of her neighbors to sit in the class to learn how they might pass the next school levy. In addition, I told her she could recruit students from the class to work on school levy campaign.

At the first-class meeting in September, local candidates from both political parties came into my campaigning class to recruit students to work hand-in-hand with their campaign staffs. Each candidate addressed my class of about forty students, and gave specifics details on the issues and expected activities in their campaigns. It was a positive learning experience for the students as they would get first-hand knowledge of what works and doesn't work in a local campaign, and the candidates were happy to get new volunteers. At the end of the first class, students met the candidates and signed up as a volunteer in one of the campaign organizations.

Rita came to the first class ready to go. She took her place up front with the candidates. Her presentation was different than the office-seekers. She told the students how much her school district had fallen behind because they couldn't pass a school levy. She gave an impassioned plea of how her children did not have the same school materials and equipment that other children had. I was surprised by Rita's ability to personalize the issues and lay out the things that the District could accomplish if they had proper funding. She was superb!

At the end of the class period Rita recruited more students than any of the candidates. From where I was sitting, it appeared that Rita's non-partisan approach was her greatest asset. She had no ideological content in her presentation. Her comments were all about what children needed and how each student volunteer from my college course could help improve the schools.

Usually, the campaigning class is divided up between Democrats and Republicans. This was the only time I had students attracted to a school levy election. It was going to be a very different campaign for them.

At the second class meeting we began with exploring the fundamentals of political campaigning. At this point every student was a member of a particular campaign committee, and they were pledged not to discuss their campaign with anyone outside of their particular political group. It was a sort of "hooded partisanship" situation as students came to class to learn about political skills and then went to their respective candidate to employ those skills.

Rita used a tape recorder in that class meeting to get any useful information that might help her cause. After class she asked if I would come to her first campaign committee meeting. She was going to chair the meeting, but she wanted me to stand by and answer questions.

Rita's "Phoenix-Talent Campaign Committee" got off to a memorable start. Ten women showed up with pencils in hand ready to learn the ropes of winning a school levy election. Rita had nearly memorized my lecture of a few days before and she laid out the plans like a real political pro. I'll never forget her saying that winning the election was like baking a cake and that she was going to give them the recipe to win the election. Her opening statement was that there are three kinds of voters in the Phoenix-Talent School District: *the saints, the sinners and the can be saved.*

First, she said were the "saints." These were the voters in the district who had supported school levies in the past. They tended to be parents with children in the schools and would likely turn out to vote in large numbers without much persuading. She said it would be tempting to spend a lot of time in these precincts because it would feel so good to be accepted, but it wasn't the best place to expend our resources. She assured everyone that the "saints" would be important, but they were not the key to winning the election.

The second group of voters Rita said were the "sinners," that lived in precincts that were strongly opposed to passing the levy. Basically, these were retired folks who lived in or near the Rogue Valley Manor up on the hill. They would likely vote against the school levy again in large numbers. She said it might be tempting to try to do the impossible by spending time trying to convert them, but it would probably be a lost cause. In fact, she said, contacting retired people would likely stir them up and activate a stronger negative vote. Our approach with the "sinners" Rita said, would be to "tip-toe around them and leave them alone."

Then she turned to the third type of voters who would be "our salvation" because these were "the souls that could be saved." Rita stressed the characteristics of this third group. They were people who had shown an interest in our schools, but in past elections they did not turn out in great numbers. Logic tells us, she said, that folks in these precincts have a lot in common with each other in terms of race, social class, income and political interests. It follows that if you turn out more of them, these newly-motivated voters will likely support the school levy.

Our task is simple, she said, find out where the "can be saved" live and target those areas with most of our attention. In past elections, "We have lost by a narrow margin, but if we find out where these voters live, we will increase the turnout and win the election. We need to go to the county courthouse and check the numbers in each precinct. Voters with high support levels and low turnout are your "can be saved." If you help them turn out in greater numbers, it can supply us with a margin of victory. She said in a loud voice: "Aim at the souls that can be saved."

Rita went beyond my lecture topic and told her committee that they were going to launch a "silent campaign" whereby they would not have any lawn signs, not do any paid media, and they would avoid doing any interviews or contact any news reporters. The telephone would be their campaigning instrument, she said. They would call friends and neighbors who were likely supporters and avoid contact with anyone else. These folks, in turn, would contact five other persons each, thus building a "telephone tree" full of voters that would surface on election day. She said it was "sort of a secret way" to conduct a campaign.

I spoke briefly at the end of the meeting and noted that the major mistake in past campaigns was the assumption that getting the most voters to the polls would help them pass the levy. In fact, it assured their defeat because voters from the Rogue Valley Manor were already motivated to vote against higher taxes. I told them it may sound "un-American," but they had no obligation to contact every voter – conducting a silent campaign would be their best chance of winning an election.

As election day drew near, I had a number of phone calls from Rita. She said they enlarged the campaign committee by bringing in more "saints" to contact other voters. The new committee members called more personal friends in the "can be saved" precincts.

She convinced the school superintendent to not send out a mail piece to the voters. He reluctantly agreed and did not do any TV or newspaper interviews. The superintendent said, "Not trying to turn out all the voters violated everything he had ever been taught," but he agreed to go along with Rita and her crew.

Election night was a happy evening for the Phoenix-Talent School District. For the first time in eight years the school levy was passed. Rita become something of a local political hero. She told me later she was going to run for the school board the next year. She called my attention to an article in the *Medford Mail Tribune* in which the reporter wondered how they passed the levy because there was no visible campaign organization.

A year or so later I saw Rita in the local shopping center. She said the school levy election had given her a new political feeling about herself. It was clear that her leadership skills were the reason why that levy was passed. She had convinced hundreds of people to try something new and it had worked.

As we parted, she said, "There's going to be another school levy election next year, but don't tell anyone." Then she smiled and put her index finger to her lips and said, "Shhhh."

EIGHTEEN

The John Birch
Christmas Party

The President of Southern Oregon College was a political sci-entist and he was also a close personal friend. We sometimes had long conversations about the state of American politics and the antics of right-wing leaders dating back to the Joe McCarthy era. But I was a bit perplexed one morning when his secretary called and asked me to come to his office. I had no idea what it was about. I didn't expect any problems, but I did wonder.

As I entered his office, I noted the absence of his usual smile and the offer of coffee. This time he was all business. He had a letter in his hand that seemed important to him. I sat down as the President read a very accusative letter that was all about me.

It began with the request that I be fired for all the damage I had done to the students and the citizens of southern Oregon. It men-tioned that I had invited Nazis and Communists on campus, and that I had a Saturday morning talk show on local radio that was "out of step with local values." There were several long quotations of things I had said. They were all out of context, but I recognized many situations. The letter was accompanied by photocopies of my course outlines with the names of persons that were invited to my classes. The guests listed were limited to a combination of Democrats and liberals. The names of many Republicans and conservatives were left off the list. The letter went on in a single-spaced format that built up the warning that the College was in "political jeopardy" as long as I was on the faculty. All sorts of thoughts ran through my head as I heard the most damning condemnation I could imagine. The President said the letter was signed by a local man over the title "Lt. Col., US Army Retired."

With a dead-serious look on his face the President said, "Now do you want to hear my reply?" I could see through the thin paper and noticed it was a very short letter. In full he wrote:

"Dear sir, I too am an Army veteran, but I wouldn't try to use the US Army to dignify crackpot political ideas." Then the President laughed and said to me, "If half of this is true, you sure have been busy."

After a while I laughed also, but I thought about that letter more and more and finally decided I wanted to meet the folks who wanted me to be fired. I knew the name of the man who sent the letter only by reputation. He was president of the local John Birch Society, a very conservative organization dedicated to exposing Communists across the nation.

One of the most outrageous claims of the "Birchers" was that Dwight Eisenhower was "a conscious agent of the American Communist Conspiracy." They believed his brother, Milton Eisenhower, was in charge of the national Communist Party, but that Dwight was the most important agent. I had read their *Blue Book* that set out their beliefs and principles. I was especially interested in their "Principle of Reversal." It was that the more someone appeared to be a patriotic American, the more likely it was that they were a Communist. The implication was that most or all the people we think are American patriots, are likely agents of the Communist Party.

I had invited the Oregon Director of the John Birch to my class. Before the class began, he mistakenly dropped a bundle of his materials on the floor in my classroom. I stooped over to help pick up them up and found he had a record of all the folks that had visited my classes. When I questioned him, he said he got some of it from the Oregon State Police, especially from the undercover agent that was always hanging around campus. He added that he had a number of pictures of me taken as I introduced various visitors to campus, including George Lincoln Rockwell, the President of the American Nazi Party, and Reverend Fred Schwarz, President of the Christian Anti-Communist Crusade. I told him that both Rockwell and Schwarz were right-wing leaders so didn't that show I had invited in leaders from both sides? He said those right-wing characters were just a "cover," that my real intention was to promote Communism.

After my conversation with the college president, I decided it was time for me to meet the local John Birch members. I heard from a conservative friend that the Birchers were having their annual Christmas Party in east Medford. I had the street address and decided to invite myself to meet the folks who wanted to fire me.

It was around 8:00 p.m when I walked up to the door. I rang the bell, but no one answered, I could hear voices inside so I decided to let myself in. There were about fifteen men and women standing around near the Christmas tree, drinking eggnog. I poured myself a drink and a man came up to me saying, "I don't think I know you." I told him my name and he gulped hard. He quickly brought over several others and said, "This is Bill Meulemans." They were all utterly surprised. At first, they just stared at me, then we began small talk about how I had found out about the meeting and why I had come to their Christmas Party.

I told them of the conversation I had with the college President and the letter insisting that I be fired. The one who sent the letter was in the small group and he admitted he had sent the letter. The retired colonel quickly noted some of the high points in the letter so the other Birchers could follow the conversation. Everyone seemed very interested.

The other members were quick to say they had heard a lot about me, but had never attended any of my classes on campus. After about an hour of more small talk, the man who sent the letter asked if I would like to attend their next meeting in Medford. I immediately accepted the invitation.

The evening meeting was at another home in east Medford. We sat around the living room drinking coffee as they introduced themselves. Each one had a short story about why they had joined the John Birch Society. Most were military veterans, but they were a different breed from the hard-core working-class folks that I met elsewhere in southern Oregon.

These were middle-class folks who dressed in suits and ties. Missing was the aggressiveness that I encountered with the guys who carried guns. There was one Protestant minister, several who said they were "business men," and the rest were retired or not willing to talk about their backgrounds. I thought I knew most of the right-wing folks in the Valley, but I knew the names of only two men in this group.

Then the subject turned to me. The first question was a zinger: "Are you now, or have you ever been a member of the Communist

Party?" I quickly assured them that I wasn't a Communist. But then there came a flurry of other questions: Why was I interested in politics? What did I think of Communist front organizations? I felt like a was being questioned by the old House Un-American Activities Committee in Washington, D.C.

At first, I thought this was kind of funny, me sitting in someone's home in Medford, Oregon, being questioned by a bunch of John Birch members. Then I began to take offense. I responded to their accusations and told them my approach to education was to provide my students with contending points of view. The goal was to allow young people to make up their own minds. One guy interrupted me asking did I think it was wise to give Communists a chance to indoctrinate my students? He said, wouldn't it be better to teach them about the Christian patriots who had "fought Communism?" He continued, "Why take a chance to let them stick a foot through the door?"

Then he asked me the names of left-wing people who had spoken on campus. My first reaction was to refuse, but then I thought I had nothing to hide. I told them that I had brought Harry Bridges into my classroom when he was in town visiting friends. They all seemed to know about Bridges; he had never admitted he was a Communist, but he was widely believed to be a member. His critics spent many years trying to deport Bridges back to his native Australia without success. Bridges was a small, feisty figure that was a well-known longshoreman from San Francisco who was involved in several labor strikes. He was the guy "everyone loved to hate!"

I told them that the visit of Harry Bridges was disappointing because he was unwilling to explain why he was a Communist nor would he even use the word in his comments. He spent all his time criticizing the FBI and the House Un-American Activities Committee that had tried to deport him back to his native country of Australia. Never in his comments did he speak of the Communist Party or his alleged membership. I told them I was certain that he did not sway anyone in the class.

Perhaps the most memorable part of Bridges' visit was that he kept track of all the members of the House Un-American Activities committee. He said when each of them died, he went to their respective cemeteries and "pissed on their graves." He said it seriously without a smile. I thought it was an example of crude humor but, the John Birch members didn't think it was funny at all.

But then I turned the conversation to the John Birch Society founded by Robert Welch, a manufacturer of candy in Massachusetts. Welch named his organization after an American Baptist missionary who was accused of being an American spy. Birch was chosen as the namesake of the organization because he was killed by Chinese Communists in 1945.

Their focus of this group from the beginning was to expose left-wing people as agents of the Communist Party. They had a long list of names, mostly in labor organizations, universities, and the State Department. There was little or no discussion of Communism as a doctrine, but only an emphasis on the danger it posed to American Christianity and the United States.

The crux of our discussion was what was the best way to inform Americans about the "dangers" of Communism. I took the position that it was important to learn as much as possible about the doctrine – that the principles of Communism had little or no appeal to American college students – that there were many contradictions built into their dogma that were easily exposed. The Birch members said my approach was foolhardy because Communists were sly and quite able to trick people into thinking that their political system favored regular people. They really enjoyed talking about how clever the Communists were – in some respects they seemed to admire them.

In my judgment, it all came down to whether we could trust average Americans to hear both sides and make up their own minds. Every one of the Birchers rejected that idea. They didn't like the idea that I trusted my student to "see through" authoritarian doctrines.

One of the men said he was a US Army veteran. I sensed he use of his status as a veteran was going to give cadence to his point of view. I interrupted him saying I was also a veteran. Then he switched the subject asking me what I thought of the United Nations. I told them I thought it was an important agency in world affairs. He went on to say that as a military veteran, he had fought to maintain our independence, and that the UN had undermined American sovereignty. They all seemed to agree that we should end our support for the UN and kick the organization out of New York City.

This reminded me of the right-wing charges against the UN made by Wisconsin US Senator Joe McCarthy. I told them the story about my home-town high school history teacher in Wisconsin being fired in the 1950s for saying that the UN was our "best hope for world peace." I recounted that a member of the local school board had said he didn't trust the UN because there were too many foreigners in the organization. None of them thought that observation was funny. They were a pretty serious bunch.

The minister in the group brought up the subject of religion and defended the Bircher methods by noting that we all need to be taught to follow God's teaching. He said it was important to get right down to talking about salvation and how "Americanism" was in support of Jesus Christ. He went on to say that the founder of their group, John Birch, had been martyred for his religion, and that it was through the blood of patriots that "America would be saved."

From here on out the conversation was laced with religion and various conspiracies about how ingenious the Communists were, but it did not contain any call to violence. Looking back on that evening, I could see that the conservatives in that group were religious/political activists that believed that there was an epic battle between Christianity and Communism. In some ways it was like a Bible Study Group where they were willing to mix their religious doctrine with a large dose of conspiracies. Their conclusion was that Communists were all around us. They were in the schools, the government, and even in our "liberal churches." They were into naming names of several people in the Rogue Valley who they thought were probably Communists, but there was no talk of using violence against them.

There is no way that the John Birch Society of that era can be compared with the violent thugs who battled the Capitol Police on January 6, 2021. The Birchers of that earlier period may have been the forerunners of the so-called "conservatives" of today, but their behavior was more civil than the present variety. In my view, they were sort of "peaceful intellectual bigots."

There was no boasting of using violence tactics among these Birchers. Their political strategy was to smear the names of their opponents, not shoot them. The Birch Society of that time believed in a traditional American culture that was Christian and patriotic. Unlike the conservatives of today, there was no mention of bombs or guns. The Birchers of yesterday may have been paranoid, but they were basically nonviolent in their approach to politics.

NINETEEN

What Could Possibly Go Wrong?

M y on-the-job training in community organizing began with Saul Alinsky, founder of the Industrial Areas Foundation in Chicago and continued on with professor Irving Goldaber, a sociologist from Brooklyn College who was called in to heal the causes of community violence in the 1970s. I soon discovered that community organizing was all about finding tactics that applied to each new situation. The strategies that worked with the Police Department of Jersey City, New Jersey, for example, wouldn't necessarily work with migrant workers on the West Coast.

The dean of community organizing, Saul Alinsky told me an organizer must speak to people through their own experiences. He said it was necessary to talk about things they already knew and understood. For example, when he was working with Caesar Chavez in California and Oregon, and he sensed that (as a Jewish guy from Chicago) he was not being accepted by Chavez and his Mexican staff. Alinsky broke the ice at dinner with the group by saying, "Do you guys eat this shit every day?" Everyone laughed as they realized Alinsky was secure enough to tell truth. They said other Gringos would choke down hot peppers and pretended they liked them. Alinsky, on the other hand, was honest. He said field workers all over the Northwest repeated the story often as proof that he was different than other Anglos.

The Alinsky story is also a good example of how an inappropriate tactic could backfire. He had a reputation as an irreverent figure who openly shocked people with his comments, but his approach would not go well with middle-class folks who wouldn't appreciate his brand of humor. While there were many universal principles of community organizing, every situation was different. Because of this, an effective organizer had the task of figuring out which tactics might work in each circumstance. It was a daunting mission for organizers who had to be able to think fast on their feet.

Generally, community organizers were advised to be careful as they searched out the mood of the people. The process of building trust was an important first step in organizing and demonstrating that the organizer understands their situation. The second step was just as crucial. It was to convince folks they could diagnose their own problem, and that they have the ability to achieve their goals. In a real sense it was the process of showing people how democracy worked.

My first work was with police departments and racial groups on the East Coast. When I returned to Oregon, I worked with groups that were as diverse as the Medford Chamber of Commerce and the Oregon Dental Association. I was in a constant search for the right tactic for each group. Sometimes a new direction came about almost by accident.

A good example of this was when dealing with the indigenous people of Oregon. In working with the Southwest Oregon Indian

Health Project, my job was to organize two American Indian tribal groups that refused to work together. We needed everyone on board to survey the health needs in a seven-county area. The head of one tribe was willing to come to meetings, but the other one refused to be in the same room with his old adversary.

Our work came to an impasse and we needed the second tribal leader to show up at a meeting. I hit a brick wall with every tactic I tried. Finally, I went to his house late one morning and found him up on his roof, patching shingles. He wouldn't answer me from the ground so I climbed up the ladder and crouched on the roof beside him. He wouldn't talk to me as I outlined the importance of the health project. Finally, in exasperation, as I was leaving, I said, "I guess you must be afraid of that other tribal leader." He dropped his hammer and it slid off the roof right beside me and hit the ground. He got off the roof without saying a word and went to the meeting. We finished the project with the cooperation of both tribes.

Usually, an organizer is not called in unless there is a festering conflict that needs to be resolved. But there were not always conflicts on campus that permitted college students to learn organizing principles. In the absence of a conflict, my students chose to organize around community improvements. For example, we decided to lobby the City of Ashland and the state of Oregon to install traffic lights on the intersection of South Mountain Avenue and Siskiyou Boulevard in Ashland. It was important to get all relevant groups on board so they could submit a joint proposal. We did the leg work, bringing in Oregon State Representative Kip Lombard, State Senator Lynn Newbry, and the chair of the Oregon State Highway Commission, Glenn Jackson. The traffic lights were installed in record time. The combined cost was nearly $90,000.

The students learned how to get something done. Every time I drive through that intersection, I think of all the work we did to achieve our goal. It was a win/win organizing project that worked. I was perhaps a bit overconfident the next time I offered the course and thought about a new project.

As I indicated earlier, there weren't always projects or conflicts ready to be resolved. One year later, after hunting around, we decided to lobby the City of Ashland to put a stop sign on Indiana Street as it intersected the east side of the campus. It sounded like an easy task, but we had to develop the issue and activate a local group to lobby the Ashland City Council.

Our central argument was that a young woman student had been hit by a car in that intersection a few months before, and that stop sign was necessary in that intersection to slow down traffic. Her injuries were serious. She had one leg amputated. We maintained this was a good reason to slow down the downhill traffic that usually went pretty fast through a crowd of students coming and going to their dorms. It sounded doable, but we encountered a big problem right away.

The first thing we learned was that stop signs are not to be used to slow down traffic. A speed limit sign could be put in, but we didn't think it would really slow down the traffic. It was a downhill slope and most cars rolling down the hill regularly exceeded the posted limit. We applied to the city council and brought in students who said they also were almost hit by a car. As citizens, the students insisted that the traffic must be stopped. In the meantime, the Ashland newspaper did a story on our project. But residents above Indiana Street said they saw no reason to put in a stop sign because there was no vehicular traffic on a cross street.

I didn't see a way around the problem, but the students thought if they applied enough pressure, and enlisted more people, the city council would relent. We scheduled an outdoor rally right at the intersection with Indiana Street. Word got out to students (not in the class) and we were confronted with a very different kind of rally. A local group calling itself *The People's Army* showed up at the rally. They had one, very threatening proposal: to immediately barricade Indiana Street with large tires with cement inside them. They interrupted our rally and called for a voice vote to put up a barricade tomorrow morning. My class members and a few other students voted against the barricade, but we were outnumbered by this new radical element. We lost control over our own project and it soon became apparent that there might well be violence as a result. *The People's Army* representative pledged to stop anyone from removing the barricade, including the police. We had a real problem!

It was late afternoon by the time I got down to City Hall. I told the city manager about the situation, but he showed little interest. I told him the proposed barricade was to be erected at 10:00 a.m. tomorrow morning. He didn't seem to understand what would happen if the police tried to remove the barricade. He looked at the clock and said, "It's five o'clock, time for me to go home."

As I was leaving City Hall, I ran into the President of the City Council who I knew well. I told him about the situation and he said, "Bill you sure are in a heap of trouble! "I'll tell you, I give you my word, we'll put in that damn stop sign, even though we shouldn't. Now you go out and tell those students that the whole matter has been settled." We felt relieved. I had a quick session with my students as we made plans for tomorrow morning.

The next morning at 9:30 a.m. my students showed up with a freshly recruited group of about 100 non-violent students. I stood on a concrete wall overlooking the intersection and announced that the city had agreed to put in the stop sign so there was no need for further action. *The People's Army* objected, they still wanted to put in the barricade. We took another voice vote, but this time we won. The crowd dispersed.

I found out later that our close brush with probable violence had come to the attention of the Oregon National Guard. Friends told me that the commander of the Medford unit was standing by, ready to order his unit to Ashland if the barricade went up. At that time there was an undercover agent of the Oregon State Police who somehow came to every meeting on campus. He apparently reported it to his superior. The undercover cop had a better attendance record in my classes than some of my students.

Afterword, we had a long discussion in the classroom about tactics in the days of radical groups that wanted to cause a violent confrontation on campus. We learned the lesson in street politics that it is important to hope for the best, but we should always prepare for the worst. It would have been our fault if the rally turned into another Kent State.

In the future we were more careful about conducting a voice vote at an outdoor rally.

TWENTY

Roosevelt and Trump

Perhaps the best way to begin this story is to reflect on a bygone era. Several years ago, I stopped off in Warm Springs, Georgia, to visit the facility where Franklin Roosevelt spent time in the natural hot spring water to build up his leg muscles after he contracted polio. I was drawn to the FDR museum and collection of photographs that spanned his life. I'd always had an affection for him even though I was only a child when he was in the White House.

It was late on a dark March afternoon as I went into the museum. There was no one else around as I went from room to room tracing the life of the man I had so long admired. It was a time of quiet reflection remembering the time of Franklin Roosevelt and the New Deal.

Suddenly I heard a muffled weeping behind me. It was an older woman behind me, across the room who was looking at pictures on the wall. I went over to her to console her, asking if she was all right. She turned around half-way and murmured, "We loved him – he meant so much to us." Within a few minutes the woman introduced herself as "Edith" from the coal country of West Virginia.

She went on to say, "It's too bad my husband Hank couldn't be with me today." (Hank had died a few months before after being a coal miner all his life.)

According to Edith, FDR saved them from total destitution with the relief programs of the New Deal. She and Hank never missed a "Fireside Chat" when Roosevelt reassured the nation during the worst economic depression in history, and during the world-wide struggle of World War II. Edith and Hank sat on their wooden kitchen chairs and looked into the small lighted dial on their table model Philco radio as they visualized the President consoling the nation as a father would comfort his children. They both realized that he helped them when they needed it the most. He was their political hero.

As they sat there by the radio, they could imagine the President plainly sitting there by his fireplace as he spoke to them in a conversational tone. She wiped a tear from her eyes as she said, "He gave us hope when there was nothing left to believe in."

Edith had a built-in chair in her walker that enabled her to sit down and tell me about her life. She said I was too young to really know how Roosevelt "had pulled the country together." According to her, there were whole families out on the street that couldn't afford the rent. She spoke glowingly of the Works Progress Administration (WPA) and the Civilian Conservation Corps (CCC) that put people back to work and gave them enough money to feed their families. "We were down and out and he reached out to us." She and her husband believed that God had sent FDR to help America, "when no one else cared." Edith went on to say that the President took them through World War II when everything seemed to be "on the line."

Edith's story summed up the feelings of love from a people who had a profound affection for a President who personalized the government by helping folks when they were down and out. Because of the crippling effects of polio, Roosevelt could not walk without heavy steel braces, but he had the strength to carry a nation through the worst economic depression in history and a world war that threatened our survival. In her mind, FDR was in a category by himself: the man that saved America.

The picture of a strong father sitting by a fireplace speaking to his children was in fact only an image. The room he used for his Fireside Chats (I found out later) was a small room, with acoustical tile, designed as a radio studio with no fireplace. But it was real to the millions like Edith and Hank who thought of him as a wise father figure that they could count on. They had an unparalleled love for the only man who really cared about them.

But in reality, Roosevelt was both loved and hated. He acknowledged the "economic royalists" who opposed him and he welcomed their hatred. FDR recognized that love and hate were at opposite ends of the spectrum, and he found that both of them were useful in building political support. That is precisely what Donald Trump did eighty-four years later.

It is common knowledge that the Great Depression provided Roosevelt with an opportunity to run as a wealthy outsider who claimed to have empathy for the folks who felt they had nowhere else to go. The FDR story is always told with the backdrop of unemployed, destitute people standing in bread lines looking for a political/economic savior. It is now clear that the Trump story will always be told also as a wealthy outsider who appealed to thousands of folks who also felt society had passed them by. The exact circumstances were different in 2016 and 2020, but the messages were remarkably similar.

Almost no one compares Trump to Roosevelt. But in Edith's home state of West Virginia, the voting response for the two candidates was very similar – FDR carried the state in four elections by wide margins, and in 2016 and 2020, the vote for Donald Trump was nearly 70 percent. Both men promised to invigorate the coal industry and put unemployed minors back to work.

The conditions in those two periods were also comparable on a personal level. Folks had lost their jobs, homes, savings, and their sense of self-respect. And most importantly, they had lost their faith in government. There was no Herbert Hoover to blame in 2016 and 2020, but Trump denounced the leaders of the establishment by name; he castigated former presidents, governors, US senators and past leaders of both parties that he said had turned a blind eye to the people who were crying out for help. Looking back, it is apparent that voters were attracted to the strength of both men, and the clear message in their campaign: "I understand your problems and I will come to your aid."

In the run-up to 2016 election, millions of voters felt that regular Republicans and Democrats had disregarded their plight – they felt ignored and angry. The feeling was that other economic and political groups were getting more attention than they deserved. In addition, long-standing social and cultural beliefs were being violated. But Trump gave them a voice as he blamed the entire establishment for all that had gone wrong. The field was wide open for a new savior who promised to tear down a system that was responsible for all that was upsetting.

Like FDR, Trump was also was a "Happy Warrior" who made fun of his opponents and swore he would make reforms that would give people faith again. It was the high point of every rally when he mocked the establishment by stating he would "build a wall" on the Mexican border and "Mexico would pay for it." When he was on stage, Trump preached a "populist gospel" of ridicule and salvation. Many followers believed him as he displayed unprecedented confidence.

Many analysts would stop short in comparing Roosevelt and Trump because they sounded so different, but if one looks deeper, both of them offered hope to people who felt they had been run over by the establishment. It is intriguing to remember that both candidates were wealthy New Yorkers who fashioned themselves as someone who understood the victims of society. Each generated strong emotions: they were adored by their followers and hated by the opposition. And after the election, both presidents had a special way to reach "their people" directly: FDR had the radio fireside chats and Trump had his twitter account until he was banned from using it. Their styles couldn't have been more different, yet the message was basically the same.

The theme voiced by both presidential candidates had three major points: jobs for the unemployed, a return of self-respect for the downtrodden, and the ringing promise to come down hard on the establishment. In both campaigns voter response was the same – they loved it!

When Donald Trump declared his candidacy in 2015, his main message was to belittle and criticize all political leaders. Moderates in both parties were at first amused by his apparent naiveté, but then they came to realize how effective he was. He said terrible things about Mexicans and bragged about himself, predicting he would be the "greatest jobs president God ever created." Many were embarrassed for him as he strutted around the stage. Political leaders in both parties and the mainstream media assured everyone that he didn't stand a chance of winning. For many, he was just a joke, but he continued to come in first at the ballot box. Seemingly, he had violated all the rules of a presidential campaign, but he kept running over his opponents in every state.

Both FDR and Trump activated a whole segment of the electorate that had been silent in their despair. Their supporters were overwhelmed by events, but they didn't know how to channel their anger. But both presidential candidates showed them how. Roosevelt railed against the bankers and the Wall Street crowd that brought on the Great Depression and he promised a "New Deal" for the country. Trump raged against the entire "political establishment" that had brought on the Great Recession and promised to "Make America Great Again." Neither candidate had specifics on how they would fulfill their pledge, but it was enough to raise the hopes of those who felt no one really cared about them.

The two candidates also benefited from the image of their opponents. FDR ran against Herbert Hoover, who many believed was responsible for the economic depression. There were many pictures of so-called "Hoovervilles," shanty towns built by the unemployed. Trump, of course, had Hillary Clinton who he referred to as "Crooked Hillary" as he charged her with a series of questionable offenses. Trump supporters enjoyed chanting "lock her up." The followers of both candidates were delighted as they listened to their man ridicule the opposition.

In both cases there were folks like Edith and Hank in West Virginia who were looking for someone who understood their plight, who felt that their way of life had been dishonored. They welcomed the fresh voice of someone who was not just a regular candidate. Both Roosevelt and Trump spoke to them directly in words they could understand.

But many things happened in 2016 and 2020 that were dramatically different from Roosevelt's time. Trump spouted outrageous things never before said in a presidential campaign. As a pompous billionaire, he made fun of disabled people, gave insulting nicknames to his opponents, belittled politicians from both parties, disrespected a well-known war hero, showed a shameful disrespect to women, and urged his followers at his rallies to attack protesters. There was also a racist element in his rhetoric. His style was provocative, but at the same time, fulfilling for his followers. Among his supporters, there were many who had never cheered a presidential candidate before. He openly attacked the entire political, economic establishment to loud cheering and applause. He hit a raw nerve among voters who felt the "establishment" had betrayed them. One older woman in Ohio – who could have voted in both 1932 and 2016 – said it was his promise to put coal miners back to work again that gave her hope.

Most observers today would not see any parallels between Roosevelt and Trump. Their campaigns were so different, but keep in mind there were thousands of folks in places like West Virginia – and elsewhere – who felt abandoned by the same old establishment. Thousands of Trump voters in 2016 and 2020 were actually descendants of FDR voters in 1932, 1940, and 1944.

Both generations were looking for someone who understood their frustration. Opposition from the establishment was considered proof that both candidates were on the side of the people. It gave folks a chance, for the first time of their lives, to take on the establishment and win.

I'm not sure whether it was a part of his grand plan, but Trump seemed to know what Franklin Roosevelt knew: that elections aren't won on issues, they are won by strong personalities who can attack the opposition. (The first rule of campaigning is to activate folks by telling them what they want to hear, and the second rule is to give everyone a chance to ridicule those in power.) FDR had more class in denouncing his opponents, but supporters in both campaigns loved to draw the line between "them and us." Mockery and scorn were powerful components in both campaigns.

Trump's comments may not have been as historically memorable as FDR had been 84 years before, but Trump never claimed to be eloquent. In this regard, he was more remindful of a backwoods preacher loke Huey Long. In a classical outsider's style, Trump told voters that the establishment had failed them, and that it was time to "drain the swamp." The pompous New York billionaire insisted again and again that he was the "only one" who knew how to "fix things." Even his obscene comments about women didn't really hurt his image. He was absolutely certain in every outrageous claim he made, (he never apologized) and voters picked up on that strength. Put simply, he could tell big lies and it didn't seem to matter. The motivating force for Trump supporters was a sense of aggressive revenge. His message was: "They had their day and now we're taking over." The content of the two approaches was dramatically different, but both presidents built an image that belonged to them alone.

Many contrasts can be made between the two presidents. Roosevelt was a liberal Democrat; Trump portrayed himself as a conservative Republican, but he had no discernable ideology. Roosevelt's main goal was to save the establishment from destruction; Trump seemed bent on destroying the establishment. Roosevelt immersed himself in building New Deal agencies that would change the nation; Trump wanted to abolish those same agencies. Roosevelt set a legislative record in his achievements during his first 100 days; Trump failed to pass any major legislation in his first 100 days; Roosevelt forged a mighty alliance to win World War II; Trump knocked down those same alliances as he isolated the US from the rest of the world. But in both cases, people correctly sensed that things would never be the same again.

Yet the two will go down in history as having left something very different behind. Roosevelt built the presidency both in size and purpose; a whole new set of federal agencies were born that changed American life in every respect; Trump hollowed out those same agencies so they were largely ineffective. FDR prided himself in uniting the country to survive a destructive economic depression and World War II. In contrast, President Trump purposely divided the country into competing segments. During FDR's tenure the United States emerged as the first super-power in world politics; Trump intentionally gave up that role and divided the Western Alliance. Donald Trump showed no interest in being a world leader; his "America First" refrain caused the United States to be seen as standing alone.

While both candidates attracted voters to their side for positive reasons, there was real evidence (in both cases) that many voters were motivated by an intense dislike for the opposing candidate. Roosevelt's opponent in 1932, Herbert Hoover, was regularly booed at his campaign stops. There was a story about a man that was attacked and beaten badly in Chicago simply because he looked like Hoover. There was a similarity in 2016 that many Trump voters were driven by their hated of Hillary Clinton. In a TV interview on Election Day, one woman in Ohio said it felt so good to vote for Trump because it was like "slapping Hillary right in the face."

Anger and fear are just as powerful as hope and enthusiasm in deciding an election. When people feel their backs are up against the wall, they are more likely to vote for a high-risk candidate that promises great change. In both circumstances some voters felt they have nothing to lose, so they are willing to gamble. But in a high-risk choice the results could go either way – saving democracy or undermining the democratic process. There's a lot of evidence that FDR tried to bolster democratic institutions, Trump, and the other hand, intentionally acted to undermine democratic principles.

After his election, Roosevelt surrounded himself with a brain trust of reformers with an idealism of saving capitalism by rebuilding the working class. Trump, on the other hand, brought in advisors with no particular vision or plan except to disassemble particular governmental agencies and reward upper-income people.

And finally, the two stories had very different endings. Franklin Roosevelt is remembered today as one of our great presidents. Donald Trump's presidential contributions are still very much in doubt.

As noted earlier, both presidents carried West Virginia by a wide margin. Now the question that needs to be asked: if Edith and her husband Hank were still alive, would they have been supporters of Donald Trump? It's possible that they would have been wearing red MAGA caps and claiming that the 2020 election had been stolen by Joe Biden. With that image in mind, it's interesting to note how people can move from the left to the right.

Maybe Roosevelt and Trump have more in common than we might suspect.

TWENTY-ONE

A Small-Town Dictator

When I was in graduate school, I ran out of money and needed to work for a year to raise enough to come back and finish my PhD degree. I hadn't considered high school teaching, but I finally came around to the conclusion that it was the best way to put some money in the bank. I had heard all the stories about how difficult it was to teach in big city schools so I chose a school out in a rural area that would not have any of the problems of an urban setting. The town's population was less than 500 people, but it drew students from a large farming area. I'll not reveal the name of the community for reasons that will be evident. But I will say at the outset that I was going to learn something about politics that I had not expected.

My wife was an experienced elementary school teacher, but I had never taught in the public schools. We drove to a small town and the school district superintendent interviewed both of us. He hired my wife to teach second grade and myself to teach junior high and high school social studies. We prepared to move into a small community that was to be our home for one year.

Shortly after the job interview the little town was in the regional news. A member of the local school board was shot and killed in the middle of a Saturday afternoon while coming out of the only grocery store in town. The shooter fired from a truck parked outside the store. Several local young men chased the shooter as he drove out of town into a field where they took away his rifle and brought him to the county sheriff's office. The shooter had just gotten out of the state penitentiary, and he said he had never been in this community before. The sheriff concluded that it was a contract killing, but no local person was ever linked to the incident. The shooter went back to prison but the identity of the person (or persons) who hired him remained a mystery.

News reporters at the time said there had been some disagreement on the school board and the man who was killed was not supported by the other school board members or the teachers. We found out later that the man who was killed had been threatened by some local citizens, but no one in town would speculate on a motive for the killing. Despite the shooting incident, my wife and I moved to the town to begin the school year.

Everything went along as planned as we arrived in town to take up our duties in the local school. The people in the town were initially very friendly. A local man offered to rent me a house at a very modest sum. It wasn't long before the other teachers and townspeople dropped by to introduce themselves. The school building was fairly new and there didn't seem to be any financial problems in the school district.

I brought up the question of why the school board member had been killed just three months before we arrived, but no one wanted to talk about it. This unsolved murder was probably the biggest story to hit this little town in decades, but no one was curious about who ordered the killing. One person said that the board member who had been murdered was supportive to the School Superintendent and also had strong disagreements about how the school was operating. I remember when this person talked about it, he lowered his voice to a whisper. That should have been my first clue that there was something wrong below the surface. The general impression I had was that no one knew (or didn't want to know) why that person had been killed in broad daylight on a Saturday afternoon. It was to remain a dark little secret that was swept under the rug.

There were thirteen teachers in the entire school. We had only about 150 students in the twelve grades. It wasn't long before everyone in the school and community knew our names. From the beginning it all looked like one big happy family. My first impression was that this was a wholesome community made up of folks who always called you by your first name.

On my first day at the school, I had a visit from the local commander of the American Legion. He informed me that I was expected to accept some textbooks provided by the American Legion. The books were all about the American military and how the military was the backbone of American democracy. I thanked him for his interest, but told him we already had textbooks for the year. He said he wondered about my patriotism. I assured him that I was a very patriotic citizen and that I had an honorable discharge from the US Army to prove it. I expect our conversation was repeated many times around town. That may have been my first mistake in the community.

From the beginning I had a very good relationship with the Superintendent of Schools. He and I had long conversations about national politics and world affairs. I thought he was well-educated and a good administrator who encouraged his teachers to do well in the classroom.

I found out later that my friendship with him had not gone unnoticed by the other faculty members and folks in the community. Many in town knew that the Superintendent had an ongoing dispute with the teachers about some practices that had been going on for more than a year. First, the teachers had encouraged the local church to hold religious services in the school cafeteria and to use the school for church dinners. Apparently, the church and the school had a "special relationship" that raised some constitutional questions. Next, the teachers were using the school truck for their personal use; one of the teachers actually kept the truck at his own home and used it for hunting trips and hauling personal items not related to school business. And finally, the teachers refused to recognize the authority of the Superintendent to furnish lesson plans for their classes on the claim that they were professionals and had no obligation to account for their actions.

Behind the scene, most people must have known that there was an unusual conflict-of- interest situation at the school. There were a couple of unusual relationships. First, the chair of the school board was the mother-in-law of a teacher named Fred who appeared to be the leader of the faculty. He was the teacher that used the school truck as his personal vehicle. Second, the mayor of the town was Fred's father-in-law. And third, I was to find out later that the constable of the town worked at Fred's father-in-law gas station, and he has afraid of being fired. Fred and his in-laws had a power triangle that was supreme: the teachers, the school board and the town government were merged together. They pretty much controlled the whole community and they had been openly critical of anyone who opposed them, including the school board member who had been shot to death.

The issue of who was in control came to a head when the

Superintendent brought up some issues at a school board meeting. He asked me to set by his side at the meeting to represent the teaching faculty. So here I was, a new person allied with a school official who was trying to get control of a community power structure that had total control over the town. It soon became evident that it was a lost cause, and that I would suffer public reticule as a result.

It was obvious at the beginning of the meeting that the Superintendent had no support on the school board. The members were unanimous in concluding that there was no need to change any school policies. The issue of the school truck, church functions on campus, and teacher independency were not even discussed. The chair of the school board, and her husband the mayor, were very prominent in the room. Everyone deferred to them.

My role at the meeting was not very clear. I just sat there by the Superintendent as his probable ally. I didn't say a word at the meeting, but I had unknowingly taken sides. I'm sure everyone noticed me sitting at the table. It was pretty much a one-sided meeting. Other people present were very quiet, but their body-language was clear, they sided with the school board against the Superintendent.

Word traveled fast outside the meeting room. While I was at the board meeting, some of my fellow teachers threw toilet paper all over my house and the surrounding trees, and they painted a big X on my front door with white paint. My house was on main street right across the street from the only grocery store where the school board member had been murdered several months before. Everyone in town knew about the incident. The next morning there was a coolness in the teacher's room that was palpable. Gone were the friendly interactions that were so common before. I could feel the cold response, but I had no idea of what was to come next.

One week later I was in the teacher's room early in the morning looking over my class notes for the day. Fred and the football coach came over to where I was sitting. Fred said, "Bill, I shot your dog this morning." I said, "What did you say?" He said, "Yeah, I thought he might chase my sheep." I got up from my chair and said, "Did my dog really chase your sheep?" He said, "Na, he was actually in your front yard. He didn't do anything, I just killed him."

The two of them just stood right in front of me waiting for me to jump up and take them on. My first response was anger, but then I thought differently. I got up, pushed them aside, and walked past them out of the room into my classroom. As the day progressed, I could feel the tension increase. Other teachers were gathering in the halls, speaking in hushed tones. I decided the only way to handle this was to work through the system.

What Fred did was wrong and I guess I wanted the law to recognize that point. Maybe Fred could be cited for damages. My dog did nothing wrong. He was just standing in my front yard when he was killed for no good reason.

After school I went to see the town constable. I told him what had happened and I asked that he follow it up by investigating the killing of the dog. I wasn't sure what could be done, but I didn't want to just drop the matter. He patted me on the shoulder and said he was sorry, but that I should be happy I didn't have any children because the same thing happened a year ago when Fred killed another dog that belonged to a person he didn't like. That time he opened the front door of the owner's house and threw the body of the dead dog onto the livingroom floor. According to the constable, the owner of that dog had a four-year-old girl who became hysterical when the body of the dog bounced across the floor. But the matter was dropped; no action was taken by anyone.

The constable offered his sympathy but added that Fred's father-in-law, not only was the mayor, but he owned the only service station in town, where the constable worked part-time. He said he didn't dare raise the issue because he was sure he would lose his job. He kept saying to me, "I'm so sorry about your little dog, I'm sure he didn't chase the sheep. Fred just does things like that."

Next, I decided to leave town and go to the county sheriff to seek his advice. The sheriff closed the door of his office when I came in. He had heard about the shooting of my dog before I arrived. He listened to my story with a look of sympathy, but he also shook his head. His comment was, "I wouldn't touch that town with a forty-foot barge pole." He said, "That's a nice place if you fit in, but they can be vicious if you cross them." He advised me to keep my head down and be careful.

I took the sheriff's advice. I took the whole incident of killing my dog as a warning. At the end of the year, my wife and I left town and I went back to finish my PhD. We left the town on good terms, but there was no going away party. I heard through a friend that the school board fired the Superintendent after we left, and later that the town turned on the minister of the local church because he didn't accept the town's leadership on a church project. I don't know whether the minister lost his dog in the process.

I had a lot of time to think through my year in that small town. It occurred to me that when a community is made up mostly of people who think, look, and act the same, there is a high probability that they would be unsympathetic to newcomers who question those in power. (I did ask a lot of questions.) There's also a tendency, in that kind of situation, for the leaders of the dominant group to feel they can get away with murder (sometimes literally). We've all heard stories of what happens to folks who don't agree to "play by the rules" in a small town.

We sometimes idealize small-town America where everyone knows each other and comes to anyone's side if there is an emergency. That may be true in most cases, but small-town politics can turn violent if someone challenges the power structure. At the time, I had no idea that my actions had made had me a target. In retrospect, I was lucky that I didn't become another victim of Fred and his in-laws. But I did take the killing of my dog seriously.

As I look back on that year, I can see that my wife and I had no real options in that town despite the fact that we lived in a state and a community where everyone (supposedly) obeyed the law. When it came down to a crunch, my wife and I were all alone. Maybe some people were opposed to the small-town dictator, but I saw no evidence that anyone had the courage to stand up and speak out. I can imagine that some of them kept their mouths shut for the sake of their families.

I was reminded of Edmund Burke's often repeated statement: "All that is necessary for the triumph of evil is that good men do nothing." In this case, everyone kept their heads down and their mouths shut. I often wondered how many other small towns were like this one.

There was no question, Fred was an enforcer who was above the law. Everyone knew it, but they didn't dare do anything about it. In this particular case, the small-town power structure prevailed, but there were two notable fatalities: the school board member who was shot and my little dog. In a real sense, they were both victims of political assassinations.

I learned a lesson in politics that year I never could have learned in a classroom. Not all the small towns are as friendly to an outsider as they seem to be.

TWENTY-TWO

Getting into The Soviet Embassy

One of the most innovative things I did in college teaching was to take a group of thirty-seven students from Oregon to the east coast on a college-credit, political science course that lasted nearly all summer. The first part of the course was an intensive period of study on campus in Ashland when we researched the places to be visited. It was called the B+1 Caravan of 1977 because it was one year after the bi-centennial celebration that had left the nation in an historical mood.

The whole operation was co-sponsored by the YMCA of Ashland. Each student was required to pay nearly $3,000 to cover all the academic and non-academic expenses including food, travel and lodging for a month-long period. I had several staff who shared in the planning and implementation of the entire project. All forty-three of us were involved in the project.

Everything was scheduled to keep costs to a minimum. We flew to New York City in the middle of the night, rented three, fifteen-passenger red vans from a cut-rate rental outfit in New Jersey, we slept on the floors in church basements, and old YMCA buildings that were scheduled to be demolished. There were a lot of meals at McDonald's.

Each day was packed with tours of historic, political places and on-the-spot lectures from myself and others. Students were required to keep a journal focusing on what they learned each day. I tape-recorded the major presentations of the summer so everyone had a recorded account of the entire course. Later, the Association of American Colleges and Universities recognized the project as being the "best summer session course in the nation."

Each stop on our course had a number of specific locations that were required. After several days on the lower east side of New York City, we went up to West Point, over to Boston, out on Cape Cod, down to Philadelphia, over to Gettysburg, down to Jamestown, up to Washington, D.C., and finally back up to New York City to catch the flight back to San Francisco and home. All told, we were on the road for more than a month. To the surprise of everyone, the whole operation went along as planned. There were no major problems.

I know Washington, D.C., fairly well and I led the three fifteen passenger red vans around the city, I tried to give the students some chances to take memorable photographs. After stopping near the White House, we were driving away on NW16th Street and passed what was then the Soviet Embassy. One of my students asked me what was that building with the red flag out front. He asked if we couldn't stop and go into the embassy. I told him it was impossible to just walk into the Soviet Embassy in the middle of the Cold War. But the student persisted. He kept saying, "Well at least you could try," so all our red vans went around the block again and we stopped in front of that imposing building.

As I was to later find out, the mansion that was the Soviet Embassy, was built in 1910 by George Pullman (of the Pullman railroad cars) as a wedding gift to his daughter. She lived there for a short time, but she died two years later on the maiden voyage of the Titanic in 1912. After the Soviet Revolution in 1917, it was purchased by the Soviet government. The building remained as the embassy until 1994, and since then it has become the residence of the Russian ambassador to the United States.

With some reluctance, I walked up to the embassy and rang the doorbell. A buzzer sounded signaling I could open the door, but I decided I would wait for a person to open the door, A middle-aged man in worker's clothes invited me into an anteroom and asked me what I wanted. I told him I was a college professor with thirty-seven students from Oregon who wanted to visit the embassy. He looked at me with disbelief and said no. I then asked to speak with his supervisor. Another man gave me the same answer. I then asked to speak to the First Secretary. After waiting for fifteen or twenty minutes, a well-dressed man in his fifties came out into the anteroom. I introduced myself and he gave me his business card. I asked again about a visit and he said in a warmer tone that it "wouldn't be possible." I then tried to sound like I was sympathetic to his government and said something about how the visit would promote "Soviet-American friendship." At that point his demeanor changed a bit. I then noticed his name on the card and asked if he was related to a man by the same name who had been involved in the 1917 Revolution. He was surprised I knew of this man who turned out to his father. Then the conversation became more accommodating. He asked if I had some identification. I handed him a pull-out set of cards from my wallet. He looked at all the ID cards and asked "What is Bi-Mart?" I told him it was an employee-owned store in Oregon. Finally, he asked, do you have any children. I said yes, and he asked their names. I told him "Cathy, Susie, and Steve." His immediate response was would I like to bring all of our group in tomorrow morning at 9:00 a.m.? I said that would be perfect.

That evening I spent a lot of time preparing the students for the next morning. I told them that the embassy was really a part of the Soviet Union, and that if they got into trouble inside, the Russians could hold them inside against their will. I coached them on being respectful and told them about the phrases similar to "Soviet-American Friendship." I didn't know what the visit might entail, but certainly it was more likely to be extensive if the students acted like they were politically interested. Everyone was going to be on their best behavior.

The next morning, we parked our three red vans on the street in front of the mansion on 1125 NW16th Street. The First Secretary met us at the door and took us up the grand staircase to a large ballroom that was decorated with pictures of leaders of the 1917 Revolution in gold-leaf frames. The First Secretary warmed up immediately to us, telling us about the building and his duties in the United States. He was very charming as he joked that he was "just a typical American suburban commuter that drove into Washington, D.C. from Springfield, Virginia every morning."

We were then led us into an auditorium where we sat in the front rows as the First Secretary answered questions. The students were great; they asked about how the "Soviet-American" relationship could be improved and what the Russians thought of President Jimmy Carter. There was also a short discussion of some Americans who had been released from Russian jails. It was a chance of a lifetime to actually met a representative of a government we had all learned to see as an enemy.

I noticed there were small holes in the auditorium walls where I imagined we could be observed. There was a stage in the auditorium and under the curtain I could see the feet of staff people who were walking back and forth behind the curtain. It was all very "Cold War" like.

As we walked back downstairs, I noticed a partially opened door on the right to a room where there were all sorts of microphones and electrical equipment. Who knows what kinds of dark things were going on in there? The front entrance had a French door with one-way mirrors so my whole conversation the day before must have been observed from the inside.

We were there for more than one hour and no one spoke out of turn. The students were so thankful and the First Secretary was so gracious. We spent most of that day talking about what we saw and heard. Later I found out that this was the only time a class of college students of any kind had ever visited the embassy. And none of this was on the schedule, but I did tape-record the session so we could enjoy it again later.

But the story didn't end there. One of the students who went into the Soviet Embassy that day later went on to the University of Oregon and received her PhD in political science. She became a professor of political science at South Florida State College where she retold the story of visiting the embassy to students in her course on American Government. A young man in her class raised his hand and told her that he knew part of the story before he ever took her class. He said his mother worked in the Washington, D.C., field office of the FBI and our whole class had been photographed going into and leaving the embassy. He said the FBI identified each of us and checked our backgrounds in an effort to find out why we went to the Soviet Embassy in July of 1977.

I found out later that it was standard procedure to check out everyone who entered the building. According to a friend of mine in the FBI, there was a constant watch on the building (day and night) to identify any suspicious persons meeting with the Russians. Apparently, it was one way to track people who might engage in illegal contacts with the Soviet Government.

The folks in the FBI must have thought we were a strange group who didn't know that we couldn't get into the Soviet Embassy. The whole event underlined one of the most interesting facts of life: that some of the best learning experiences happen by accident.

TWENTY-THREE

The Poor People's Conference

We all know that we learn the most in situations where we are personally involved so I wrote simulations that placed my students in roles that required them to think and act in circumstances that were as realistic as possible. The theory was they would gain a personal understanding of politics that couldn't be duplicated in any other way.

I wrote a simulation game that set up a fictitious situation that pitted the poor people of the state against Oregon state government. It was a highly emotional topic in which people in the simulation made statements that would go far outside the bounds of regular politics. The whole simulation was built on a fictious situation in which state welfare payments were being reduced by 10 percent.

The focus was on what welfare recipients would do if state payments were reduced by a significant amount. I anticipated that several students in the class would have personal experience in receiving public assistance payments and that they would add a note of realism to the simulated activities. On the following pages is the printed material given to the students:

Recipients from throughout the Oregon have converged on Salem for a weekend of meetings and discussions with state officials concerning a proposed reduction in public assistance payments from the state. The group of about 800 men and women are being housed in several school gymnasiums on cots and sleeping bags, and they are being fed at public expense.

Leaders of the welfare group contend that the payments have been cut by massive amounts. All discussions center around the proposed welfare schedule which was circulated for the first time last week. The standard monthly grants for the coming year have been revised in the following schedule showing the former and proposed figures in real dollar amounts:

Former Number in Household	Proposed Grant Schedule	Reduced Grant Schedule	Sum Per Household
# of persons	$ amount	$ amount	$ amount
xxx	xxx	xxx	xxx

Most of the welfare recipients had come to the conference in an angry mood to find some way to restore the payments to the previous level. State accountants estimate that the budget would be more than $17 million dollars out of balance if the earlier payments were restored. Leading state economists are united on the need to reduce state welfare payments.

Federal welfare funds have been exhausted for the year. The question has been reduced to two choices:

(1) Restore welfare payments to the previous schedule at the expense of many basic programs in the state, or

(2) Hold the line on budget cuts in all state departments including the Department of Human Services.

Leaders of the state legislature and the governor have sympathized with the public assistance clients, but they stood firm on the position that all budgets in the state must be trimmed to accommodate the loss of revenue for the coming year. One veteran state legislator summed the position of the state:

We all have to tighten our belts during the recession to balance the budget. All state employees are unhappy with the outlook for next year, but they just have to bear with us. Just yesterday, representatives from the Highway Department contended that they really needed an increase to maintain our highways at present safety standards. Members of the State Board of Higher Education came in last week and said they feared nearly irreparable harm to every university in the state. The list goes on and on, but we can't play favorites. If we restore welfare payments to their previous levels, many state employees would receive drastic cuts in their salaries, and over 2,000 jobs would be eliminated so the budget could be balanced. I know it will be difficult to live on the reduced sums. We may be able to do something about it later if revenues pick up during the year. Presently, we are looking into the possibility of shifting some of the welfare costs to local churches and civic groups. Perhaps it might be better if local charities could help solve some of their own community problems.

Just weeks before the conference, the state legislature proposed a new tax package which would cut personal income taxes and corporate taxes in an effort to stimulate the sagging economy. The entire tax plan will be referred to the people for a vote next month. Most major economic groups have endorsed the tax reform. It is expected to pass by a wide margin.

Spokespersons at the welfare recipients conference are

well aware of the economic situation, but they maintain that the new welfare schedule is completely unacceptable. This is the second downward revision of welfare payments in recent months. The general feeling in the group is that the present level is far below poverty standards, and the new lower level of payments would endanger the health of thousands of children across the state.

A welfare mother from Portland brought the conference to a standing ovation when she declared:

I will not stand still while the state reduces my family to the status of a public liability and an economic problem to be resolved by local handouts. We cannot exist on crumbs thrown to the poor and still maintain a decent home for our children. Why should you and I go home quietly and accept this starvation status when there are public employees at the upper level in the state who are making $200,000 a year? If the state needs more money, why don't they raise income taxes on those people who ride around in big cars? We have a right to live just like everyone else. Other people in the state receive payments and subsidies from the public treasury without a stigma. Why do we have to beg to receive money to feed and clothe our families? I will not let my children go to bed hungry just so this state can balance their damn budget. This is serious! If we don't get a restoration of just and equitable payments, I say we should go down fighting. If the governor and legislature don't answer our plea in the next three hours, let's move into the area around the buildings and break every window we can find!

At this point a large group of welfare recipients begin milling around the many state buildings on the capitol mall. The mood of the crowd is angry. Some protestors have brought in bricks from a nearby construction site. Undercover members of the state police on the scene conclude that loss of life and property is imminent if a solution is not found in three hours. The pressure builds as everyone searches for a solution.

Please read the positions of the following three roles and assign yourself to one the groups. Private meeting rooms will be provided for each group:

1. Welfare Advocates: Those who press for action in a crisis situation. Your grievances provide a Advocates focal point for the conflict. You should feel close empathy with powerless people in despair. As an advocate of the poor people throughout the state, their case is your case. Keep in mind in accepting any compromises, there are thousands of people depending on you.

2. State Officials: Those who hold the official role of spokespersons for the governor and the Officials legislature. You have the power position to yield or hold fast to the poor people's demands. By virtue of your position, you will receive the brunt of the protest. In your capacity as a decision-maker, you have dual concerns that are in conflict: balancing the state budget versus rising welfare costs.

3. Mediators: Those who represent the classic third party that are technically neutral and beholden to none in the dispute, but possessing values and commitments which can influence a peaceful outcome of thc crisis. Your major effort should be to develop a strategy for a solution, and to gain a commitment from both sides to end the conflict. You have a free hand to contact both groups during the negotiation process.

Group Meetings

Each group has the responsibility to maintain their integrity by probing and challenging everyone's right to be a member. The following questions should be asked every person who seeks membership in the group:

1. Why did you choose this group?
2. What special background do you have that qualifies you to be in this group?
3. Why should we vote membership to you?

The success of each group will depend on the strength and character of each member. Situations may arise when an in individual will represent the group. For this reason, it will be necessary to purge out persons who are only mildly committed to the group's mission.

A majority vote will grant permanent group membership. All others will be asked to leave the room. Do not vote for persons who have not proven themselves to your satisfaction. Those persons expelled my seek membership in another group, or watch the simulation without becoming involved. After a short strategy session, each group will decide to make its first move in the process.

Your instructor will abdicate control over the process. He will play the role of a newsperson with a recording device that may be used to send proposals between the groups. The situation is in your hands.

My Analysis of the Self-Selection Process

First of all, each student had the freedom to choose a role that reflected their political character: The question was: are you a poor people's *advocate*, a *state official* or a *mediator*? The underlined words in each category were a short-hand description of each person's political self-image. The role of each person was set.

They were to engage in a self-selection process that really answers "What kind of person am I?"

1. Do I feel a strong empathy for poor people in despair?
2. Do I see myself as a person who can take charge and maintain an orderly process?
3. Or am I the kind of person who can bring folks together and settle a dispute?

Things I Learned in the Self-Selection Process

In a class of forty or more students, there were at least six or eight students who had a direct, personal experience with being on welfare. It might have been a parent, family member or even themselves. The questioning of people in this group turned out to be the most important factor in the entire simulation. The *Welfare Advocates* were the only group that insisted on members having a background of understanding of what it was like to be poor. Secondly, I discovered that the *State Officials* group attracted folks in my class that were police officers in real life, those who majored in business, prelaw, law enforcement, or any one of physical sciences. And thirdly, the campus politicians were drawn to the *Mediator* role along with many political science, sociology and history majors.

Group Meetings

The *Welfare Advocates* had the most dynamic process in the entire simulation. The members were all women. They told their personal stories of what was like to be a single mother on welfare or how their own mothers didn't have enough money to feed the family. Some of them talked about going to bed hungry when they were a child. Each personal story seemed to bring them closer together. They discussed the public shame people feel on welfare.

They broke into tears as they discussed the personal agony of being poor. The advocates were careful to exclude anyone who did not have a gripping personal story to tell. I stood in the back of the room and watched the cohesion of this group. I was also aware that no one spoke about compromises in this group. They were cemented together by leaders who built an emotional bond that reflected their personal experiences. This was the key process for the entire simulation. The advocates focused on the subject of poverty and refused to compromise with anyone else.

The one thing none of my students knew was that simulation was designed to fail.

The *State Officials* didn't really know what to do. A couple of police officers talked about how important it would be to work through the system. Individuals sought membership by indicating that they believed in obeying the law. The group did not refuse anyone that sought membership. This turned out to be the largest group in the simulation, in part, because the members didn't have a clear set of expected action.

The state officials thought they had power. But they were to find out, this was not the case.

Mediators were a smaller group made up of students who really thought they had special skills. But like the *State Officials,* they did not refuse anyone from membership. A couple of mediators started looking at the payment schedules and proposed a couple of possible compromises that could be taken. After about forty-five minutes, they asked me to take their proposals to the advocates. But by that time the advocates were in no mood to bargain. For them the simulation had crossed the line into a confrontation that only they understood.

Mediators thought they could ease the conflict. In fact, they had no chance at all.

Unexpected Individual Reaction

I organized this simulation on a Friday/Saturday seminar during the summer session. I used rooms in the Student Union with doors that could be shut. There was a clock in the foyer that everyone could see. The three-hour deadline put pressure on everyone. The first two hours went by fast as the poor people's advocates fed on each other and became more committed than ever. The *State Officials* and *Mediators* did very little, but everyone was watching the clock.

It wasn't long before everyone caught on to the fact that the advocates were running the entire simulation. In the last hour, this group of eight women were closer together than ever. Their eyes were red from crying. Their determination was growing. They went outside and brought in rocks that they said would be used to break nearby windows. No one knew if they were serious. There was a distinct possibility that they would break some windows in the Student Union. Tension mounted. I must confess that I was concerned at this point. Everyone was watching the clock.

By this time the *State Officials* and *Mediators* were standing by wondering what was going on. One of the state officials was completely confused, he kept saying, "Why are these women so serious, this is only a simulation?" At this point there was also a complete lack of understanding as to why the *Welfare Advocates* were crying. Other students couldn't comprehend their unwavering commitment as the advocates huddled on the tile floor beneath the clock with rocks in their hands. As the three-hour deadline neared, there were other students and Student Union staff persons who were looking on wondering why a group of eight women were knelling on the floor shouting, "We won't give in, our children need food to survive"

Then came the surprise. As the second-hand swept up to twelve, the women banged their rocks on the tile floor making an eerie sound similar to windows being broken. At this point, some of the *State Officials* and *Mediator*s began to cry as well. Everyone was completely exhausted as the class session ended on Friday afternoon. Students wandered away in small groups.

It took time for all of this to sink in. On Saturday morning the class met at 9:00 a.m. for a wrap-up of the simulation. There was a strange cohesion in the room. Gone were the roles that they had played the day before. Now there was a combined seriousness and silence that I don't think I've ever encountered before in a class of forty people. They all realized what had happened yesterday and how close they had come to some form of violence. The *Advocates* were quiet and almost withdrawn because they had borne their souls in front of everyone. The students from the other two groups were consoling the advocates with words and looks of acceptance. There were tears around the room as everyone shared their emotions.

I had about forty-five minutes of taped messages on my "newspersons" tape recorder. I spent a couple of hours on Friday evening editing it down to about twelve minutes. On Saturday morning I played the edited tape consisting of short statements that everyone could recognize. The tape was a clear indicator of how fast things got out of hand – of how the personal experiences of the advocates could polarize a situation – how the *State Officials* and *Mediators* had no chance to deescalate the process. There were more tears around the room as everyone listened intently.

After playing the cassette tape, I decided to give the edited version to the woman who had led the *Advocates*. Her voice was heard again and again. Everyone applauded as I gave her the tape. Her strength had kept the *Advocates* together and brought the simulation to a head that no one could have foreseen. The class broke up with a kind of silent awareness that the students had entered a situation that was fraught with danger. What would have happened if the rocks had been used to break windows? No one knew, including me.

The leader of the *Advocates* was on a high as she realized her own sense of power and leadership in the simulation. Later I found out she gleefully played the tape for her husband, who was the city manager of a nearby city. The husband did not share his wife's pride. He said, "What in the hell are they doing over there at the college? Why are you shouting on this tape?"

The argument about the wife's role in the simulation ended weeks later in a divorce. Certainly, there must have been other factors, but the unexpected individual responses of students convinced me that the design of this simulation was both valuable and dangerous. I decided I had no right to set a process in motion that could get out of hand and cause emotional and physical damage. There may have been some modifications I could have made to the simulation, but it would have been difficult to build in safeguards while retaining the dynamics that made it such an effective teaching tool. The underlying question is how much should a simulation uncover behavior that could lead to violence? I thought a lot about my role in bringing this about.

I did not use this simulation again for the reasons already stated. No doubt a similar simulation of this kind could be written to demonstrate the destructive power of racism. It could feature the aftereffects of the killing of an unarmed Black person. In a sense we have all watched dynamics of this kind get out of hand on our television screens. In some respects, it's the unforeseen simulation story of twenty-first century America. It turns out that there are all these powder kegs are all around us. We have all seen them explode on our TV screens.

This simulation taught us a lesson of how politics can escalate quickly and get out of control. In this particular case, the prior welfare experiences of the women were the key ingredient. While the simulation was fictious, their prior experiences were real. This group of eight women built a commitment that none of us expected. We should have been aware that there are thousands of American citizens who are carrying around pent-up anger that could explode at any times.

It was only a simulation, but there was a taste of real life with all the volatile qualities we have in American politics today. That's one of the reasons why politics is so unpredictable.

TWENTY-FOUR

Doing the Right Thing

S erving in elected state office should be simple. In most cases it boils down to making decisions that are good for the community being represented. But what happens when the people want something that is not good for them? Does the electorate have the right to violate public health standards through a public vote? Should a state representative ever vote to approve a measure after the people in the legislative district have soundly rejected it at the polls?

That was the situation in the Rogue Valley in 1984 when the Oregon Department of Environment Quality (DEQ) warned the people that the levels of local pollutants in southern Oregon were damaging the lungs of folks, and that it was going to be necessary to clean up emissions from motor vehicles, wood stoves, and local industries. The DEQ measured levels in southern Oregon that were worse than large metropolitan areas across the nation. There were many days every year when the valley was in violation of the Clean Air Act and public health was clearly in jeopardy.

The Rogue River Valley is unique geographically because the whole area is shaped like a saucer with mountains on all sides with and a very low wind velocity inside. During the winter months especially, there were several days when there was no wind and there were double and triple air inversion levels whereby the pollutants were trapped at the ground level producing a smog that was one of the most unhealthful in the nation. Everyone knew there was a problem, but there was a strong resistance to the regulations necessary to remedy the situation.

The DEQ was charged with establishing plans to reduce pollutants and bring the valley into compliance with national standards. Folks in the Rogue Valley were given the chance to vote on the new regulations. They turned down the plan by an overwhelming vote. The major concern was that new regulations would require motor vehicles in the valley to be tested, and if they failed the emissions test, they would need to be repaired at the owner's expense. The so-called proposed Inspection Maintenance Program (I&M) was exceptionally unpopular. Scores of people pledged they would fight anyone who forced them to have their cars tested. Also in the threatening measure were air quality standards for small particles in the air and other pollutants coming from wood stoves in the region. Folks were worried that they would not be able to use their stoves during the winter when air pollution was at its worse. Voters in the rural areas of Jackson County were especially angry about the proposed measure.

The negative vote in southern Oregon did not alter the air quality situation. The state of Oregon was required to establish air quality strategies to resolve the problem. The state legislature had little choice but to bring the issue to the floor for assured passage. Southern Oregon legislators were under tremendous pressure to vote against it even though everyone knew it would pass.

The Oregon House of Representatives had a sufficient number of votes for passage of the measure. The Democratic leadership in the House knew it was a very controversial measure in southern Oregon so they informed Ashland's State Representative, Nancy Peterson, that she could be excused from the vote, thereby avoiding the charge that she had voted against the will of the people.

The day of the vote, Nancy Peterson considered taking the pass. She told me later that she sat in her office by herself after hearing fellow legislators advise her to leave the building and avoid committing political suicide. No one would criticize her for taking the easy way out. After all, she could say that it was a program that her constituents had rejected by a large margin so she had no other choice.

In a personal conversation later, Nancy told me she was still unsure as she left her office and entered the elevator. She placed her finger on the button that would provide her a way out of the building, and she could say she wasn't present that day. But then she moved her finger to the button that would take her to the floor of the House where she would be required to indicate her position on the measure. In the end Nancy went on the floor and voted for the measure.

Nancy Peterson told me later that she had to "do the right thing for the right reason." She voted for the I&M program and regulations on wood stoves knowing it would anger thousands of voters who would gear up to oppose her in the next election, but it was necessary for public health. All of this went through her mind as she destroyed her own political future by her own hand.

So why would Nancy do such a thing when she could have taken a different route that would have been approved even by her liberal friends as "something she had to do for her own political survival?" She told me that the reason her finger pressed the other button on the elevator was because of her "conscience." I remember saying to her, "Couldn't you say you were just following the will of the people?" She hesitated and said to me, "That's the wrong question." The right question she contended is, "What should I do when I knew what was good for the people?"

I admired her when she supported the I&M and wood stove measure, but I knew she was going to be in trouble on election day. It was big news all around Oregon, especially in her home district where there were a lot of folks who thought she had betrayed them. Yet she went out doing door-to-door campaigning. She didn't duck the rural areas where the negative I&M vote was almost 80 percent. She tried to talk to people and convince them that the I&M requirement was necessary. Nancy Peterson had a lot of doors slammed in her face. She told me one woman said, "Oh, you're that bitch that voted for the I&M. I'll never vote for you for anything."

Every public opinion poll we did during the late summer showed her losing by a slender margin in District 52, but we cheered her on. She had a majority support inside of Ashland, but the response in the outside area wasn't even close. The poll numbers declared that she was going to lose. I think all of us on her campaign committee were prepared for defeat. Her Republican opponent had a great advantage because there was an iron-clad anti-Peterson vote out there that would not change no matter what happened.

Election Day 1984 dawned clear and cool. It was a presidential election year and a large turnout was expected. I had a position as a television commentator in Medford on election eve, talking about voting trends and totals that showed who was ahead in each race. It was so difficult to present the voting results when I felt personally involved. As expected, Nancy was running behind all night long. It wasn't by much, but she never had the lead. My job was to talk about probable reasons for the apparent upset that was in progress.

I had to mention the I&M as the big issue that was dragging Nancy Peterson down. The last voting results from the Jackson County Elections Department showed Nancy behind by the thinnest margin of the evening. As I remember, it was less than 100 votes. I was certain that it was the I&M measure that was causing her defeat.

My wife and I were members of a five-person committee that ran Nancy's campaign so we were both heartbroken by her apparent loss on election night. But my wife had a dream two nights earlier about another outcome. She dreamed that Nancy won, but that she didn't know about it until after she went to the Capitol in Salem, and that a Portland television station showed a TV screen image of her learning of her victory while taking on the telephone. In the dream my wife saw Nancy shouting, "I won! I won!" The dream didn't make sense. Neither my wife nor I took it seriously. We agreed it couldn't happen that way. Political leaders don't win an election after they go to the legislature. It seemed ridiculous.

The day after the election I called the Jackson County Clerk to find out if the absentee ballots had been counted. She said they had not been counted, but that we shouldn't have any hope because the absentee ballots usually favored Republicans. But I thought there was still a slim hope.

In the meantime, the Democrats in the Oregon House had an early meeting in Salem to make plans for the upcoming session. Thus far, twenty-nine Democrats and twenty-nine Republicans had been declared elected. There were two House seats that were too close to call: Nancy's seat in Jackson County and another seat in Klamath County. The Democratic House representatives were meeting in a closed-door session to consider all their options. They left word with the staff that no one should interrupt their caucus meeting inside the Capitol building.

Late that afternoon the Jackson County Clerk completed the vote counting for House District 52. She called us in Ashland and said Nancy had won by, as I remember, seventeen votes. We immediately decided to call Nancy in her Salem office, but we were told she was in a caucus meeting that could not be interrupted. Then we called another number to a pay phone located in the hall just outside the caucus meeting. My wife told the staff member who answered, "Listen, I have some news for Nancy Peterson that she will want to hear. She will want to talk to me. I want you to go into that meeting and have her come to the phone out in the hall."

The staff member finally went into the meeting and brought Nancy out into the hall. Apparently, Nancy had an excited look on her face. Seeing this, the Portland TV camara crew anticipated some news as they turned on their lights and cameras just in time to televise Nancy answering the phone and exclaiming in an excited voice, "I won! I won!" The unlikely dream had come true. She had done the right thing for the right reason and the people re-elected her. A recount was done and she hung on to one of the slimmest margins in Oregon political history.

Nancy Peterson continued her career in Oregon politics until she was diagnosed with a very severe form of cancer. By this time, my wife and I had moved to the Portland area, but Nancy called all five of her campaign committee to come back to her home in Ashland where she was near death. The five of us stood around her bed. She could see that all of us were uncomfortable so she broke the silence and gave us direction. She said, "You all planned my campaigns, now I want you to plan my funeral." A few days later she died.

We organized Nancy Peterson's memorial to be held at the largest room on the Southern Oregon University campus at the

Student Union. We invited all the Democratic and Republican officials from all over the state. Many people spoke that day, but I remember most of all the comment made by one of Nancy's two daughters. She said Nancy loved to read the girls bedtime stories but sometimes she "adjusted the endings." In addition to everything else, Nancy was a strong feminist. The girls said if the story had anything to do with males and females, Nancy would change the ending a bit so the females came out well in the story.

At the memorial we had an overflow crowd of all the people she loved and who loved her. She was one of the few politicians that was truly loved in a bipartisan manner. Even some of her foes on the I&M issue respected her at the end because she always did the right thing for the right reason. Many times, later, I've wished we would have more leaders follow her example.

"Doing the right thing for the right reason" should be a guide for all elected officials, but even in cases where it has been the guide, it doesn't necessarily assure victory at the polls. Next is the story of one of the most famous Oregon political figures who had a reputation for always "doing the right thing for the right reason," but in this case, it led to his downfall.

TWENTY-FIVE

The Conscience
of the Senate

O regon's Wayne Morse was one of the most politically unpredictable US Senators in American history. He went through three political party designations while in office. He was elected as a Republican in 1944, but dropped out of the GOP in 1952 to become the only Senate member of his Independent Party. He finally joined the Democratic Party in 1955, where he remained until he was defeated by Bob Packwood in 1968.

While in the Senate, Morse infuriated five presidents on a regular basis: Roosevelt, Truman, Eisenhower, Kennedy, and Johnson. Each of them complained that they could never count on Morse to support the party's position on the Senate floor. He angered leaders of both political parties when he crossed over and campaigned for members of the opposing party. His favorite slogan was "principle above party" and it fit him well in everything he did. But despite his reputation as a maverick, he remained a progressive throughout his lifetime.

Perhaps Senator Morse's most famous and controversial stand was his intense opposition to US involvement in the Vietnam War.

He was one of only two US senators who voted against the Gulf of Tonkin Resolution in 1964 that gave President Lyndon Johnson a free hand to widen the war in Vietnam. Morse repudiated the US policy on Vietnam at every opportunity. He openly accused LBJ of mounting an "unconstitutional war" in South East Asia. Oregon's senior senator was exceptionally unpopular with those who said he was not supporting our troops in Vietnam.

Despite the criticisms, Morse had a confidence in his foreign policy pronouncements that bordered on arrogance. He was like an aggressive attorney as he piled up evidence that overwhelmed the jury of public opinion. I remember how impressed I was every time every time I heard him speak. He could convert an audience to his point of view within minutes.

It was clear that Morse loved being a US Senator, but he seldom relaxed in the role. Though he often smiled when he spoke, it was the smile of one who feels superior and looks down a bit on his contenders. Some of the harshest criticisms he made were made against his fellow senators. I remember listening to Morse in the Senate Foreign Relations Committee in Washington, D.C., where he referred to his fellow senators by name for their "pussy-footing around" on American foreign policy. Other members of the committee typically looked away when Morse got into one of his tirades. The Senator from Oregon lectured everyone, including the Committee Chair, J. Willian Fulbright of Arkansas, who admitted later that he was greatly influenced by Morse's views on Vietnam.

In my memory I never saw anyone intentionally take on Wayne Morse. His opponents thought he was a bully, they criticized him behind his back, but they didn't want to stand toe-to-toe with him. There was a defiant quality in his temperament that made other senators withdraw when he was around. But Morse seemed to enjoy being independent of other senators. It was not uncommon to hear him taking a liberal position on education, labor, civil rights, consumer affairs, and the rights of women with no one standing beside him. He often spoke on the Senate floor at the end of the day on a subject that others ignored. He had a reputation of being a man of passion and commitment. Everyone knew where he stood on nearly every controversial issue. The media called him "the Tiger of the Senate."

Unlike other political leaders who usually had a few drinks after a busy legislative day, Morse didn't drink alcohol and was not at ease telling jokes or stories. Some Senate colleagues referred to him as "Typhoid Mary" because very few people warmed up to him. He didn't attend the "after hours" sessions in the US Senate where many decisions were made. While other senators were engaged in political chatter, Morse was busy doing research. He seldom stepped out of his role as the self-appointed "conscience of the Senate" with the implication that other Senate members were not so principled.

But Wayne Morse's reputation in Oregon was strained. He enjoyed strong support among professional educators and labor leaders, but they also complained that he was unpredictable. He interceded in several management and labor disputes, sometimes upsetting his friends in organized labor. He told a long-time labor leader, "You can support me, but you can't own me."

Everyone knew Morse was his own man, and it was a delight to see him appear on television programs like Meet the Press where he would interrupt the questioners and lecture them on why the president was subject to congressional control. His favorite point was to declare that American presidents did not deserve support if their positions were contrary to the US Constitution.

Democrats in Oregon were divided on Wayne Morse. They

either loved him or hated him. He was admired by all the critics of the Vietnam War and folks who supported his liberal positions on domestic policy, but many partisan Democrats were completely turned off by the Morse's criticisms of Lyndon Johnson's policy on the war in South East Asia and his endorsement of Republicans who supported his positions on foreign policy. Oregon Democrats were seriously divided on the topic of Wayne Morse.

It is tempting to explain Bob Packwood's victory over Wayne Morse's defeat in 1968 as due to the obvious factors: Morse was a sixty-eight-year-old politician with a raspy voice who was known for his never-ending opposition to the Vietnam War. Packwood was a fresh thirty-six-year-old moderate with no political baggage. The clear message was it was time to retire the old man and bring in a fresh face who put Oregon's interests on the top of his priorities.

All of the above reasons explained why Morse lost the race, but there was more to the story that reflected the unexpected factors in the campaign. Morse seriously underestimated his opponent. Packwood told me he reached out his hand to Morse at a public function in the early part of 1968. Morse shook Packwood's hand without recognizing him, but pulled his hand back when Packwood identified himself by name. The story was told many times as evidence that Morse didn't know anything about Packwood and didn't care; he never took him seriously.

In addition to Morse's lack of focus, there were several underground factors that came into play. Packwood won the Republican nomination in 1968 without a serious opponent so he had the freedom to speak unopposed at service clubs and club meetings across the state. People began to notice this young, bright candidate as a good choice to replace an aging Wayne Morse. Packwood spent a lot of his time building his organization, setting up campaign captains in each community. He had a long list of young professionals, Jaycees and other folks who had attended his own political conference at the Dorchester Hotel in Lincoln City on the Oregon coast. "People for Packwood" was an upbeat, optimistic group who were eager to get involved in the 1968 campaign.

I spoke to Wayne Morse in May of 1968 when I introduced him at a campaign rally in Medford. I asked him about Packwood, but he waved off the question, saying that he trusted Oregon voters to make the correct choice. In his remarks that day, he said he had a secret political weapon, "the fact that Oregon ranked near the top in literacy ratings across the nation." He rested his case on Oregon voters being able to read and understand the issues. Morse spent nearly all of his time that day speaking about the Vietnam War, and how Lyndon Johnson had violated the Constitution by sending American troops into battle without a declaration of war.

As the campaign rolled on. It was clear that Morse was becoming an "one-issue candidate." I had friends who said they were getting a little tired of being told that it was an "unconstitutional war." Opinion polls were showing that the race was getting tighter as time wore on. The senior senator had met his match, but he was still was not paying attention to the Packwood organization.

I recall watching a Packwood event in front of the Jackson County Courthouse in the fall of 1968 where his volunteers were preparing to go door-to-door in Medford. Before they left the staging area, a group of about twenty of them paused to sing the National Anthem with real gusto. I'm not sure if this was a normal part of their preparation, but I do know it seemed to give them a psychological boast like a football team going back on the field after the first half to win the game. Wayne Morse had nothing in his arsenal to compare with the perky, young professionals in the Packwood campaign.

I had students working in both campaigns. They collected political materials and recorded their activities in their respective campaigns. Students who worked for Morse spoke of the lack of leadership in the campaign. On the other hand, the "People for Packwood" organization may have been the best organized campaign in recent Oregon history. They had materials that provided volunteers with a suggested message for telephone and door-to-door work. The enthusiasm of the Packwood volunteers created an excitement that was new to Oregon politics. They were a happy group who believed in their candidate.

The media side of the campaign also showed a contrast. Packwood cut some powerful thirty-second TV spots that featured well-stated quotes from a recent debate with Morse. There was an entertainment value in the Packwood commercials – they were fun to watch. The Morse spots spoke of his seniority in the Senate, but I doubt many folks understood why seniority was that important. He tried to use psychedelic colors in his ads, but they looked like they were done by a shady ad agency. Packwood's ads focused on the young candidate with an upbeat personality.

Morse appeared in his ads to be an old war-horse trying to look like he was hip. Oregon voters choose the young man with the upbeat personality. To the surprise of everyone, Packwood won by a margin of less than one vote per precinct.

But since that time, history has been kind to Wayne Morse. Fifty years later, his contributions to political affairs seem almost prophetic. He is remembered for being ahead of his time on issues that included the War in Vietnam and the danger of presidents who acted without restraints. His switching of political parties, when viewed from today seems heroic. Wayne Morse may have been argumentative, but he was truthful on issues involving the future of America. If he were in the Senate today, there would be no doubt that he would have been the major voice in the Congress against the wars in Iraq and Afghanistan.

There is often an underground factor in politics that amplifies political character. Those who do things for the right reason as Wayne Morse usually did, often have a political legacy that grows after they are gone despite their onerous nature. Perhaps the United States needs a Wayne Morse type in Congress to lecture us about the lack of constitutionality in American foreign policy. History has a way of going to the bottom line of political leaders: "Did they do the right thing for the country?" Later we tend to view a man like Wayne Morse in positive terms.

"Doing the right thing for the right reasons" may be simplistic statement of purpose, but it may be one of the best assessment tools we have to build a legacy in politics.

TWENTY-SIX

What's It All About?

I was a member of the politics faculty at The Queen's University of Belfast during my eleven years in Northern Ireland. My lectures and other campus duties were all on Mondays and Tuesdays, so I had the rest of the week free to do face-to-face research with the working-class people of both religious traditions. Most of my time was spent in the small sectarian neighborhoods of Belfast where there were unsightly twenty-five-foot walls dividing folks of the opposing communities. There were more than eighty specific localities in Belfast that were identified as being either totally Catholic or Protestant. Some were small embattled areas that have been invaded by the opposing side, so folks were careful to guard against a dangerous situation that might arise at any time of the day or night. Each neighborhood was like an armed fortress. Everyone had a watchful eye.

I spent a lot of time getting to know folks on both sides of the divide. I found them to be exceptionally friendly because I was regarded as a neutral person with no ties to either community. I was able to move freely without too much concern for my own safety. I soon developed the habit of having a camera slung over my shoulder as an indication that I was an outsider, perhaps a tourist who was just looking around. After spending a several years in Belfast, I found I had more friends there than I did back home in Oregon.

I soon got to know the routine of the sectarian neighborhoods. Protestant and Catholic children went off to separate schools each morning. They all wore school uniforms so it was easy to tell them apart. More than 90 percent of the children went to schools that were identified with their particular nationality. The Irish Tricolor flag was out front of the Catholic schools and the British Union Jack identified the Protestant schools. Most of the children never had a chance to interact with kids from the opposing community. They lived an isolated life where everyone stayed in their place.

After school, the children often engaged in the low-level sectarian activities by throwing rocks and bottles over the neighborhood walls. Even though they never met the kids on the other side, they all had sectarian nick-names. Much of life seemed like a staged rehearsal to reinforce membership in their own tribe. Stories were told on each side that focused on how "different" they were from "us." Each side had their own cultural traditions complete with their own mythology, history, music, football teams, pubs, social clubs, political parties, and paramilitary armies. The street curbs were painted red, white, and blue in the Protestant areas of town and green, gold, and white in the Catholic neighborhoods. Everyone grew up in a highly structured environment with no appreciation for what life was like on the other side.

I visited many schools in both communities and discovered that the elementary and secondary schools in Northern Ireland were an important part of the socialization process. In the absence of personal experience with folks from the other side, there were a lot of half-true stories that were repeated again and again. Everyone knew the terrible tales about the "enemy." A person was born into a religious tradition and was expected to stay there for life. They could have a full life of seventy or eighty years and never develop a relationship with someone from the other side.

The first "acceptable contact" between the two groups was at The Queen's University of Belfast where I was on the faculty. But the integration didn't really occur there either. In my course on American politics, I had students from both communities, but I soon discovered that the Catholics sat on the left side of the lecture hall while Protestants were on the right.

On campus there were disputes on whether to play God Save the Queen at graduation ceremonies. The Catholics refused to stand up when the music was played. The Protestants quickly reminded everyone that this place of higher learning was called "The Queen's University." Later the university officials compromised by playing the European national anthem, *Ode to Joy.*

Some of the governmental officials came up with plans to break down the sectarian division between young people. One of the earliest efforts was to sponsor a football (soccer) game so the boys might get to know each other on the playing field. This was tried only once because both sides saw it as a chance to attack each other on the field. I knew one young man who was involved in the one and only first game. He said, "We nearly kicked each other to death before they pulled us apart."

Then the government sponsored combined school class trips to visit a museum or planetarium under the supervision of teachers from both sides. This didn't work well either because the children didn't even want to be in the same room. The opposing mythology was so strong that they were reluctant to stand together or make contact on these trips. Each peer group set down a fairly clear border between the two groups. No one dared to cross over and make friends.

Finally, an organization was formed that took the children out of Northern Ireland in bipartisan pairs and sent them to the Netherlands where they spent a few weeks with a host family. The initial reports were favorable. It was found that Catholic and Protestant teenagers could get along reasonably well as roommates as long as the peer group weren't involved. But a problem arose when they came back to Northern Ireland and found they could not continue their friendship because they would be beaten up if they crossed the sectarian boundary line into each other's neighborhood.

I became involved in the process and served as a board member on *The Northern Ireland Children's Holiday Scheme*. The plan was to take a small, mixed group to the United States to see if they could forge friendships that might last when they returned to Belfast. A lot of planning went into the project. The British government funded the program.

I brought over a group of fourteen teenagers (seven from each tradition). There was an equal number of boys and girls that were fifteen and sixteen years old. They flew from Belfast to Portland where I took them to their dormitory rooms at the University of Portland. A Catholic priest at the university agreed to supervise their overnight times on the campus while I was in charge of their daytime activities. Surprisingly, the Protestants thought the priest was a great guy because he bought them a pizza. It all worked very well.

Our group of fourteen teenagers spent a good deal of time around Portland, visiting places that would interest young people their ages. I tried to take them to see things that would be outside their experiences in Belfast. We went to Timberline Lodge on Mount Hood and to the volcanic visitor's center at Mount St. Helens. But perhaps the most "educational day" was a visit to the Mexican-American Cultural Center in Cornelius, Oregon. Cornelius was about 50 percent Hispanic and it is located about twenty-five miles west of Portland. It was planned as a chance to become aware of the cultural diversity in Oregon, but surprisingly the visit turned out to be a "test" on whether the kids from Northern Ireland really understand their own conflict back home.

There were about an equal number of Hispanic and Northern Irish teenagers in a large room. I introduced the session with a short statement about the Northern Ireland conflict and an invitation for questions from both sides. At first the questions were general in nature, like "What is your neighborhood like?" or "What is the weather like there?" But then an especially articulate young Hispanic man asked, "What is that conflict in Northern Ireland all about? Why is there so much fighting in Belfast?"

To the surprise of everyone, the combined group of Protestants and Catholics couldn't come with a good answer. At first, they said, "We just can't get along with each other," and then the point was made, "We really hate each other." Then there was a moment when the young Mexican seized the moment and said, "Why are you killing each other?" There was more stuttering and repeating the same general comments about how the two sides have been fighting for hundreds of years. To the surprise of everyone, the young Mexican-American kid became a bit more assertive saying, "You really don't know do you?" There was a silence in the room. The Catholics and Protestants from Belfast were very uncomfortable. They didn't have an answer.

In the fifteen-passenger van going home that afternoon, they were unusually quiet. None of them turned on the radio to listen to rock music. They just sat there looking out the window. When we stopped, I asked them to take a break and talk about their session with the Mexican-Americans and their inability to explain the conflict. They said they "didn't know where to start," that there were "so many things, we couldn't put our finger on the real reason." Then the topic turned to what they should have given as the reason. But they still couldn't come up with a real answer. It was beginning to upset them. They said no one ever asked them that question like that before.

One of my colleagues at The Queen's University of Belfast told me one day: "The conflict in Ireland is about everything and nothing." The "everything" relates to all the mythological factors that cover nearly everything in life. The "nothing" refers to the fact that the major issues are so ill-defined that they are nearly impossible to articulate. The important point was that the working-class people of Belfast can't tell you why they are so obsessed with the conflict, but it remains as the most important issue of their lives.

For me the high point of that whole trip from Belfast to Portland was the visit to the Mexican-American Cultural Center. I played the verbal exchange through my head many times as I remembered the uncomfortable teenagers from both communities of Belfast. When I got back to Northern Ireland, I shared the story with both Catholic and Protestant adults. They just shook their heads, but they didn't offer an answer either.

In more recent times I've been wondering how a group of American adults would do if they were questioned about the cultural conflict in the United States. How would they respond to the question, "What's it all about?"

What would they say about then so-called "big lie" in American politics? How about folks who refused to take the Covid vaccine for political reasons? Would losing your freedom by wearing masks in public come up? What would be the explanation of why the red and blue people are divided on American school boards?

It may be instructive for us to know that the Northern Irish didn't have any of problem with the issues cited above. The Catholics and Protestants of Belfast acted much more rationally to the Covid-19 pandemic than did many people in the United States. The folks in Belfast may have harbored 800-year-old sectarian attitudes, but they believed in science.

The last time I was in Northern Ireland I noticed an improvement in community affairs. The walls were still there, but there was a growing openness among the embattled neighborhoods. When I came back to US, I noticed things were getting worse. The United States was becoming more like the old Belfast where there was a tension in the air that no one could explain.

The conflict in the United States is becoming more about "everything and nothing." It's about all sorts of things that turns folks against each other, but underneath it's about "nothing you can put your finger on." Maybe it's time to take small groups of adult Americans to Belfast where they could get away from the irrational things that divide them.

I wonder what they would say if a northern Irish kid would ask them, "What's it all about?"

TWENTY-SEVEN

It Keeps Good Time

During the 1950s I was in the US Army stationed in West Germany near Frankfurt. One afternoon I was roaming around a part of the city that had many small shops with used items that were for sale. I stopped at one shop and noticed a wrist watch that was for sale for the equivalent of just a few dollars. It was gold-colored with a brown leather band. It was slightly discolored but it was set to the correct time. It was an old-style watch that needed to be rewound every day, but the price was so low I decided to buy it.

In 1956 I returned to the United States to begin college. My second-hand wrist watch continued to serve me well as I finished graduate school and begin my college teaching career at Southern Oregon College in Ashland, Oregon. I replaced the brown leather band with a matching extension band but the watch continued to "keep good time." On a few occasions I considered buying a new watch, but the old one worked well so I decided to keep it.

In the mid-1960s I began offering an evening course titled "Political Extremism in America." One of my students came up after my evening class and we started talking about people who had unusual talents. She told me her mother could determine the character of a person by holding an object that had been with that person for a long time. She said, for example, if you gave me your watch, I could take it home and she would reveal things about yourself that you might find interesting." I remember thinking I didn't want to be without a wrist watch for a few days, but my student was very persuasive. I've always been interested in people with these kinds of talents so I gave my wrist watch to my student. She promised to bring it back at the next class meeting.

A few days later my student brought back my watch. She put it on the lectern in front of the room, but she didn't stop to tell me anything about her mother's reaction to the wrist watch. At the end of the class meeting, I questioned her as she was leaving the room. I had to stop her at the door to find out about her mother's response to the watch. The student didn't seem to want to talk about her mother, who she said was not feeling well when she held the watch. My student apologized saying she was sorry but she had nothing more to tell me.

The whole matter of the mother being sick and the student's unwillingness to talk about the incident struck me as strange, but I was to find out more when the student's mother surprisingly came to the next class meeting. The mother came up after class and told me she was relieved when she sat through the class meeting. She blurted out, "I was so wrong about you, and I am so happy to see that you are so different than your wrist watch."

I didn't know what to say, yet I wanted to know more about the watch, but the mother was the one who started asking questions: "How long had I had the watch? Where did I get it? Had I ever thought of getting rid of it? I answered all the questions, but I concluded that "it kept good time" and I didn't see any reason to get rid of it.

The student's mother actually pleaded with me. She said when you leave this building, "find a place where you can throw it away where no one will ever find it." She raised her voice and proclaimed, "That watch belonged to someone who did terrible things." The mother continued, "I was actually afraid to meet you tonight, but I know now that you have no association with that watch." She repeated herself again and again. "That's a bad watch, get rid of it."

It was a very emotional evening that left me wondering if that watch did have some "qualities" that I did not understand. But I'm a practical guy. I didn't notice anything wrong with it, and I remember thinking to myself "it keeps good time." I was perplexed and I wanted another opinion before I would throw away what I thought was a "perfectly good watch."

A week later I went to an informal faculty party on a Friday afternoon after classes were over for the week. One of the faculty persons was a former Catholic nun who had a special teaching position in the Psychology Department. Somehow the conversation came around to the subject of unexplainable events. I told everyone there about my incident with my watch and my student's mother who demanded that I throw it away. The former nun expressed an interest and asked me to give her the watch. She put in on her wrist for only a few seconds. Without warning she took it off and threw it across the room. She exclaimed "I feel terrible things. People are dying!" Other people in the room were shocked by her reaction. There was a long silence in the room as the subject was changed to a topic that had no relations to the wrist watch. I went over and picked up the watch and put it back on my wrist.

A month or so later, I was visited by one of my former students who came back on campus to tell of his accomplishments. He had just gotten married to a woman I did not know, but the three of us went to a bar near campus to discuss Oregon politics and the upcoming general elections. My former student asked me how things were going, and I immediately thought of the recent experiences with the wrist watch. I told him and his wife about the string of unusual reactions and his wife asked if she could see the watch. I handed to her and she put it on her wrist. I turned away to talk more with my former student. After about fifteen minutes or so, the former student asked his wife, "What are you doing? What are you writing?"

I turned around and found that his wife had filled several napkins with a hand-written message. She had the watch on her wrist and she seemed to be in a daze. She did not look up when we spoke. Finally, she just broke into convulsive tears. Her husband was visibly shaken. He kept saying, "There's something wrong with her. I've never seen her act this way."

I asked to see the three napkins she had filled with her written comments. I could see all the words written clearly in English, but none of it made sense. The husband said he couldn't understand it either. Then she read her own words out loud and began to weep again. She was so embarrassed and wondered if we thought she had lost her mind. The three of us sat there for the next half hour, reading and rereading the words that appeared to be entirely random. I felt so sorry for her because she said over and over that I must think she was crazy. When we parted I asked if I could keep the napkins. My former student and his wife left. I did not hear from them again.

I showed the napkins to several faculty members and none of them could understand the significance of the words that were strung together. One of my colleagues taught a course in linguistics.

He bragged that he could understand anything written by any person. In this case, he failed because, he said, none of the words made up any sentences. Even the commas and periods appeared to be in a random order.

After a while the story of my watch spread around campus. Those who saw it were disappointed because it looked like any other older watch. One of our secretaries told me I should take to a person she knew in Medford who earned her living as a psychic. She supplied me with a phone number and an address in West Medford. I called to make an appointment and I showed up at a very modest house near the Medford industrial park.

The woman held the watch for a few minutes before she began to ask me the same questions I had heard before. Where did I get it? How long had I owned it and if I had any idea where it may have come from? The psychic was not surprised that I had gotten the watch in Germany. She said it belonged to a German man who had been involved in World War II. She commented that he had "no sense of empathy for anyone," and had no concern for "what happened to other people." The psychic said she could see many buildings inside a fenced-in area. She seemed certain that the person who owned the watch had something to do with the Holocaust. Later she told me that there were images of "defenseless people" in her mind. She wasn't certain if the man who owned the watch was involved in killing people, but she was certain that the operation didn't bother his conscience at all. She said I should immediately get rid of the watch.

I didn't take her advice but the watch would soon be taken from me. It was during the summer of 1977 when I took a group of 37 students to the East Coast. We were near the end of the trip. My son, who was then six years old, had wanted to use the men's restroom in a Virginia state park in Alexandria. It was a hot day and I took off the watch, put it on the counter and splashed cold water on my face. After a few minutes, my son and I left the restroom and I noticed my watch was missing. There were no other people in the area that might have taken it. We spent a half-hour looking through the restroom and all waste containers. It was gone!

I had mixed feelings when I lost the watch. After all, I owned it for twenty-two years, but there was another part of me that felt relieved. I can't prove it, but I felt my life had turned a positive corner when the watch was no longer in my possession. And I also discovered that my new watch kept good time as well.

Since then, I have come to believe that everything happens for a reason, that nothing is an accident. With that in mind, I have tried to understand why this happened to me. What significance did the watch have in my life? I still don' know.

TWENTY-EIGHT

Lennie's Hopes and Dreams

One of the fringe benefits of living in Ashland, Oregon, is that there are world-class theatrical productions just down the street. The Oregon Shakespearean Festival has been performing there in a beautiful setting for more than eighty years. Each year theater-goers flock to Ashland from all over the country. The festival not only presents the works of Shakespeare, but great American plays as well.

My all-time favorite production was *Of Mice and Men* by John Steinbeck. I had read the novel long ago and was looking forward to seeing the play. Despite my familiarity with the story, I was struck by the local presentation. There was something about the actors that gave me a new insight into a deeper meaning into this classic tale.

Almost everyone knows the story-line of the Steinbeck's book. It is a colorful account of two migrant workers, Lennie Small and George Milton who wondered around northern California during the Depression doing farm work. George was a very capable man and Lennie was mentally disabled. The two had been together since they were children. George was the one who made decisions while Lennie followed along like an obedient child. The situation was compounded by Lennie's large size and his simple-minded approach to life. Lennie loved to say, "I'm strong as a bull," but the problem was Lennie didn't know his own strength. There were occasions when George had to rescue Lennie after he injured other people.

It turned out that Lennie's strength was a two-edged sword. The two were able to get work in the fields because Lennie could do the work of several men, but George was always worried that Lennie might be provoked and would hurt another person and the two of them would be on the run avoiding the consequences of Lennie's actions. Other men would often taunt and make fun of Lennie, not realizing his tremendous strength. It was always a source of tension in the story.

Even Lennie knew he could become a serious trouble-maker. There was an agreement between the two of them that Lennie should hide out after he did "a bad thing," and George would come and find him and they would run away together. There was a kind of love between the two of them with George in the parent role and Lennie as the child that could easily get into trouble.

But from my perspective, the enduring message of the story was Lennie's hopes and dreams that he and George could save up their money and someday get a "place of their own" where Lennie could "tend the rabbits," and where they could be their own bosses and say "to hell with the work" anytime they wanted and just stay at home. Lennie recited his dream again and again. He said repeatedly, "Tell me again George about how it will be when we get our own place." George would repeat their vision of the future, but with a noticeable doubt in his voice that the day might never come.

Then came an event that involved me in the story! One day I

was driving out of Ashland going west toward Medford when I was surprised to meet a car on the road with a small pile of cards flying off its roof. I guessed immediately that someone had unknowingly placed their open wallet on top of the car and drove away. Then I took a quick look at the driver and said out loud to myself, "It's Lennie driving the car." For a moment, I wondered if someone in his mental condition was able to operate a motor vehicle.

I made a U-turn at the first opportunity and chased after "Lennie," blowing my horn until he pulled over to see why I was trying to get his attention. I rushed up to his car and told him about the cards that had flown off the car. Together we went back and picked up the cards that were scattered all over the road. He said "thank you" over and over while all I could do was to tell him how many times I had seen *Of Mice and Men.* But I still couldn't get rid of the idea that someone like Lennie could actually drive a car.

It wasn't long before Lennie introduced himself as the actor, John Norwalk, who played the part of Lennie. After we picked up the cards, John suggested we go for a cup of coffee.

For the next hour we sat in an Ashland restaurant and discussed the Lennie role and what the story was all about. I soon discovered that John Norwalk and I had the same views on what Lennie represented: It was all about how all of us humans are driven and inspired by our hopes and dreams. John said he often "teared-up" on stage when he asked George to "tell me again how it will be when we get our own place." As we sat in that café, we both identified with Lennie and the promise of finding our "own place" in life where we could be happy.

There was a meeting of the minds that stirred us both. It was like fate had been waiting to introduce us so we could share our own "hopes and dreams." The more I talked to John Norwalk, the more I could understand that he had reason to search for his "own place." He had been a captain in the US Marines and had served as a combat officer in portions of Vietnam where there had been fierce fighting. He said the memories of Vietnam gave him a type of mental disability that reminded him of Lennie. John said that his role in Vietnam had "twisted his dreams" so much that he wondered if he could ever be happy. I could see that John had invested himself in the role of Lennie at a personal level and that his passion on the stage had made the role come alive for the audience. John said that this role was like no other in his career.

Then our conversation turned to what happened to him one day in the final scene of the play. It grew out of a situation on stage in which Lennie had accidentally killed a woman at the ranch where he and George were working. It was Sunday afternoon and the ranch-hands were busy playing horseshoes while Lennie was alone with a woman who didn't realize that she was getting herself into trouble.

Lennie was always attracted to soft things. This time it happened to be the woman's hair. As he grew more aggressive in petting her hair, she began to resist. Lennie didn't know how to react when she tried to get away. He became confused and grabbed her by the neck. The result was that he broke her neck. Lennie immediately knew he had done "a bad thing" so he ran away to a secluded area waiting for George to come and find him. The final scene opens as George finds Lennie who, by this time, is babbling about how sorry he was for doing "a bad thing."

Lennie completely lost control of himself at this point as he started thinking the trouble he caused may have endangered their goal of getting "their own place." He was down on his knees gushing out tears as he gazed out over the audience giving the impression that he could actually see the rabbits out in front of him that he wanted to pet. There was a child-like look on his face as he peered into the distance as he imagined what life could be if they had "their own place."

But George was aware that the other ranch-hands had found the woman's body and figured out that Lennie had killed her. George knew if they caught Lennie, they would might torture him and maybe even hang him. Now George had to make a terrible decision. The audience could see that George had a pistol and that he had to kill his best friend to shield him from the lynch mob that was bearing down on them. George was standing behind Lennie as he held the pistol to the back of Lennie's head. But Lennie was still unaware of the dire circumstances as he continued to talk about the rabbits and how it would be when they got "their own place."

In one dramatic instant, the sound of the gun shot echoed through the theater as the lights went off leaving everyone in total darkness. The audience was struck by a profound silence, but one teenage boy in the audience laughed. It was probably the laugh of an immature boy who couldn't handle his own emotions, but it affected John Norwalk with instant anger.

John told me that his immediate plan was to stand up as the lights came up and address the boy who laughed and explain that George had killed Lennie out of love, and the whole scene was to illustrate that sometimes good people had to make terrible decisions. But the actor that played George grabbed John Norwalk's neck and held him down until Norwalk realized that the power of the play was that both George and Lennie left the stage in the dark so the audience would have a moment to understand that killing Lennie was indeed an act of love.

After a few more months, *Of Mice and Men* closed in Ashland.

John Norwalk moved to Seattle where he assumed a new acting role. At Christmas time, John called me to touch base one more time as he drove through Ashland on his way to visit his parents in Arizona. The day before New Year's Eve there was a short article in *The Ashland Daily Tidings* that John Norwalk had been killed in a one-car accident on a sunny day in Arizona, and that he was to be buried in the Willamette National Cemetery for veterans, a few miles southeast of Portland.

I knew immediately that I had to see John one last time. But when I arrived in Portland, I was told it would be a "closed casket" service because John's body was badly damaged. I decided to play a role myself that would enable me to see John once again.

My PhD degree entitled me to be called "doctor." I never used the title, but I decided in this case posing as a medical doctor might get me into the backroom of the mortuary. I introduced myself as "Doctor Meulemans" giving the impression that I had something to do with his body after the accident. I was permitted to see John Norwalk again who was laid out in his dress-blues as a captain in the US Marines. It was at that moment that I surveyed the chain of events: first my focus on the stage play *Of Mice and Men* – then the cards that flew off John's car – our shared views of Lennie's hopes and dreams – the realization that we, ourselves, were inspired by our quest to find "our own place" in life – and finally John's death. I realized that all of this didn't just happen by accident.

I remember looking down at John and wondering if he had found his "own place" in death. In some way I thought the story ended there, but in another way, I was still alive seeking my "hopes and dreams" so the play continued.

TWENTY-NINE

Surviving a War

When I first arrived in Israel, I was sent to a small Kibbutz by my scholarship hosts to get oriented and to get rid of my jet lag. I was alone the first day as I entered the dining hall. Seated at the next table was a group of older folks who I discovered were all Holocaust survivors. They gathered there together once a year as guests of the Kibbutz. The project was funded by the German government as a part of the reparations after World War II.

It wasn't long before the survivors invited me to join them as they recalled their many personal experiences in the death camps. I apologized for asking so many questions, but they said they wanted me to know more so I could go back home and tell their stories. It turned out that I spent nearly all my time in the dining hall as their guest for several days. They encouraged me to take notes.

They told me so many stories about how they survived. One woman, for example, told of her escape from a train en route to the camp because, as a teenager, she was small enough to fit through a small window near the top of the railroad car. Other persons lifted her up to the window and she fell head-first outside the moving train along the road bed. She landed on sharp rocks and was cut up in the process. Some neighboring farmers took her in and tended her wounds. She was proud to say that she spent the rest of the war working with the resistance in Poland sabotaging railroad lines and bridges.

A man gave a gripping account of how he carried thousands of bodies out of the gas chambers to the furnaces where they were cremated. He did it all-day-long for two years. It still bothered him that all of those people died while he was selected at random to survive. He said the memories of the dead reappear nearly every night in his nightmares.

There was a sense of obligation with all of them at the table to tell their whole stories with all the graphic details. Every word was a part of a gruesome history that the Jewish people will never forget. All the conversations were memorable, but there was one story that still brings tears to my eyes.

Hannah had been a middle-aged Jewish house-wife that lived in Poland with a disabled husband and a five-year-old daughter. Her husband had been an accomplished musician that had played a viola in the local symphony orchestra, but he had suffered a stroke that ended his musical career. Hannah took care of her husband and her five-year-old daughter, who was her pride and joy. Everything in the household revolved around the little girl.

The three of them were poor, but Hannah scrimped and saved to keep everyone looking respectable. She spent a lot of time making a new coat for her daughter. It was made up of large and small patches of cloth that ordinarily wouldn't go together in a coat. Hannah said no two buttons of the coat were the same. Nothing matched. The finished product was unlike any other coat ever made, but the daughter loved it because it was the only new piece of clothing she had ever owned.

The family received a letter in the autumn of 1940 from the German authorities that occupied Poland. They were told to be ready at 9:00 a.m. on a date next week to be relocated to a new place. Hannah said she spent several days cleaning the house. She didn't know who might occupy her house in the future, but she didn't want to leave a mess behind.

At nine o'clock sharp the German soldiers showed up with two trucks. Hannah and her little family were standing outside waiting. Hannah didn't know where they were going, but she made certain the three of them were dressed in their best. This was especially true of the daughter, who was wearing her new coat. The husband was holding his viola because it was his most prized possession, even though he could no longer play it well.

The first thing the soldiers did was to take the viola from the husband and smash it on the street. The husband fell to his knees crying, trying to pick up the little pieces to put it back together. One of the soldiers said, "You won't be needing that where you're going." Next, they grabbed the daughter and father and put them on one of the trucks that drove away. Hannah was left standing alone in tears. Her questions and protests were ignored as they shoved her onto the second truck.

She discovered later that the Nazis considered the father and daughter unfit for any work, but Hannah was able-bodied and fit for labor. She never saw either of them again.

Hannah looked at me when she said, "They destroyed my family and there was nothing I could do." I recall everyone at our table was in tears as Hannah described her time in the camp. Her job was to sort out the clothing of the Holocaust victims who had been gassed and cremated by the Nazi authorities. There was a separate pile for men's, women's and children's clothing.

I think everyone at the table knew what was coming next. None of us could hold back tears as she described the day she found her daughter's coat. Hannah told us in great detail how she held the coat in her arms and wept. She had hoped beyond hope that maybe her daughter might have survived. She wondered if her husband was with her child in their final moments. No one, of course, could answer her questions.

Hannah said there is still a part of her today that thinks there may have been a miracle, that her daughter might have somehow survived. As a mother, she could not accept the absolute fact that her daughter was dead. She added, "I still keep track of her today. I know how old she would be. I celebrate her birthday in my own quiet way." On occasion, Hannah said, she sees a young woman who, she imaged, might look like her daughter if she were alive. She added, "I dream about her often. I can't forget my little girl.

After my time at the kibbutz, I had many opportunities to meet with people of all ages who were involved in memories of the Holocaust. I also had contact with many Israelis who discussed their current relationship with the Palestine people. Therein was a problem I had not anticipated.

During my time in Israel, my senses as a human being was under attack on a daily basis. On the one hand, I could hear stories like the one from Hannah, but I could also hear accounts of discriminatory policies toward the Palestinian population in this country. It was contradictory information about the same people in a very different situation.

This was partly due to my preferred daily schedule. Without exception, I spent my days with the Jewish people and government officials in Jerusalem. During the afternoon and evening hours I was able to catch a ride of about twelve miles to visit some

Palestinians I had come to know outside of Ramallah. Personally, I was subject to a back-and-forth treatment that I could not reconcile. I was well aware of the "security problem" in Israel, but some of the things I heard about and saw went far beyond the need to maintain security.

One evening I was having dinner with a Palestinian family who said they were having trouble economically. They had lost their farm when it was seized by the Israeli government in the 1950s. They were given no compensation for the farm. They took the matter to a court and were told the farm was occupied for security concerns. The family members could not accept the judgment of the court. An older member of the family went by the farm and picked some fruit off trees planted by his grandfather. He was arrested and charged with trespassing on his family's own farm. He was forced to pay a small fine for the fruit he took home to his children.

Another case involved a different family outside of Ramallah who raised chickens for a living. They were forbidden to sell the chickens and eggs because it would be in competition with Israeli farmers who were also chicken farmers. The Palestinians renovated an old cave for their "illegal" chicken farm. They took me into the cave to see their chickens who had never seen the light of day. I was told that the police would kill all the chickens if they ever found out.

The war in Israel today is taking a toll on everyone. I was introduced to an Israeli man named Amos who was born in Wisconsin. The most noticeable feature about him was a black patch over his right eye. It turned out that the loss of his eye had changed him politically.

Amos had been raised in Milwaukee, Wisconsin. He had immigrated to Israel to help build what he called the "Jewish homeland." By his own admission, his family had raised Amos to believe in the goodness of humanity. His mother and father were both physicians back in Wisconsin. "We were," he said, "Jewish liberals to the core." But all that changed when Amos was compelled to serve in the Israel Defense Force (IDF).

The story goes that Amos and another Israeli soldier were surrounded one night by young Palestinians who were using slingshots to shoot ball bearings at them. The other soldier fired at the gang of young people to keep them as a distance, but Amos hesitated. He said he just couldn't shoot at another person. The result was that the attackers got close enough to hit Amos. He was blinded in his right eye by a ball-bearing.

With a look of anger, Amos looked at me and said, "Liberalism was my weakness." Since then, he said, he has come to recognize there are a lot of people out there who will hurt you if you give them a chance. Amos said he was converted to a new political point of view out on the battlefield in an instance. He said he "thinks differently about a lot things" since his injury. The political hazards of life have transformed the way he thinks. His view of human nature changed in an instant. By his own admission, he moved from the far left to the extreme right. Amos said he is raising his children to fight back to defend the family. His story may have application to many families who live in a war zone.

What happened to Amos reflected the experiences of many Israelis who were raised in a leftist environment with an emphasis on humanistic values and culture, but then came the experience of living through a war. Nearly everyone was required to serve in the military. It was difficult, if not impossible for them to defend their Jewish state while fighting an indigenous people who also claim that same homeland. It's hard to be liberal and care about the humanity while carrying an AK-47 for personal protection.

Again, I started thinking about parallels in the United States. I feel uncomfortable when I'm at home in Oregon around persons who are armed with assault weapons. Unlike Israel, we have no need to carry an AR-15 while walking down the main street in Oregon communities. But more and more I see folks showing up at political meetings with semi-automatic weapons. The laws in some states are changing to permit more people to carry guns in more places like schools, grocery stores and taverns. The murder rate and school shootings keep rising as more people feel the need to buy assault rifles and other weapons of war.

I don't see how this story will end well.

THIRTY

The Cross-Hairs
of Our Rifles

A fter a few years in southern Oregon, I had worked up quite a reputation for being a professor who would bring anyone on campus to speak about any subject. I actually enjoyed that designation because I kept the campus open to people who would normally not have access to the academic community. We set up a series of public meetings on campus for visiting political leaders and local people who had something to say. It was called, "Experiences in Politics," and it wasn't long before we had a steady string of folks who were outside the boundaries of two-party politics.

There was a great variety of speakers that ranged from the Black Panthers to members of the John Birch Society. It was also a forum for Oregon politicians who wanted to launch their campaigns in southern Oregon. I encouraged my student to attend the speaking occasions. The media was regularly involved in publicizing the campus events. Many of the proceedings were televised. The local press was always informed of these events.

One of my students worked at a local radio station. He and I did a couple of interviews about local politics and he asked if I might be interested in doing a weekly call-in radio show. It wasn't long before I started a three-hour Saturday morning program on KYJC in Medford. It was one of the most interesting experiences of my time in the Rogue Valley.

The radio program was great fun, but I didn't realize at the time that it was the first of its kind in conservative southern Oregon. Before then, all the media outlets had been rather careful not to stir up the right-wing opinion makers that dominated the area. I guess I didn't appreciate how deeply embedded the quasi-military culture was in southern Oregon and northern California.

I soon discovered that some folks liked to talk about guns. Not just the kind hunters use, but big guns, the kind used to disable armored vehicles. Some callers said that federal officials did not dare come to their particular communities because they had been warned to stay out. I'm not sure if that was true, but the Rogue Valley seemed to be way ahead of the rest of the country in terms of forming armed militias, collecting firearms, and storing ammunition. The "right to keep and bear arms" was like a religion to these folks.

I had one man who called in and boasted that he was ready to take on federal officials if they came to his place. According to him, he had twelve anti-personnel mines buried around his farm. They were placed in areas where federal agents might walk to approach his house. One of his problems was that he had to get rid of a couple of steers he had because he was pretty sure they would set off the mines, but he didn't think his dogs would detonate them. He said he also had an alarm set up that would go off when anyone drove up his driveway. That particular guy only called in once. I wondered if anyone ever set off his land mines.

On my radio program, I regularly had calls from folks who were anti-UN, anti-Semitic, anti-Black, anti-intellectual, and most of all, anti-Communist. I'll never forget the program when I indicated that there were members of the Communist Party in Ashland. The callers were shocked. One man kept saying, "Do you mean they're living right here in the Rogue Valley? They also asked about academic tenure and whether I had that designation. Most of them thought it was a system that protected "disloyal college professors who undermined American values." But it would confuse them when I invited them to come to campus to speak or to be interviewed in one of my classes. I made it clear that everyone had a right to be heard.

The radio call-in program had a fairly large audience. On occasion, some people wrote letters to the editors of local newspapers. They quoted the radio conversations in some detail, suggesting that there was a lot of controversy on the program. In addition, I received many angry phone calls at home. The program took up more and more of my time.

I regarded the call-in show and the contacts made as being my own kind of research project because I taught my Political Extremism in America every fall for twenty-seven years. I always had a fresh insight as to what was going on in right-wing America. Surprisingly, some of the folks who called in became my friends.

During the time I had the program, I was invited to countless right-wing meetings in churches, private homes, and public places. People didn't think I would show up, but I nearly always did if I had the evening free. Virtually all the meetings were designed to promote fear. The theme was, "The threat is more serious now than ever before and it's getting worse." I made it a point to never disagree with the people I met. My purpose was to listen and take notes.

As the program progressed into the late 1970s, some members of the audience became more aggressive in their accusations and defense of right-wing views. There were more calls and anonymous letters to my home. As time went on, the number of personal threats increased. Some reminded me they knew where I lived and what route I used to walk to campus.

One Saturday morning a caller provided a detailed account of the killing of Alan Berg, a radio talk-show host in Denver. Berg was shot twelve times with an illegal automatic weapon as he got out of his car in his own driveway. The Denver talk-show host had angered members of The Order, a White nationalist organization that killed him because of his liberal attitudes voiced on station KOA, a 50,000-watt station in Denver. This particular caller didn't threaten me on air, but it was clear that he wanted me to know what happened to Alan Berg.

Shortly after being told of the Berg case, a local, unnamed organization sent a neatly-typed letter to my home outlining the patriotic mission of their group. The envelope was postmarked in Medford. The letter warned me that members of their group lived "nearby," and that I would never know if one of their members was the "mail carrier that came to my home," the barber who "shaved my throat with a straight-edged razor," or the garage mechanic that could "file down the tie rods on my car." The letter closed with the warning that, "The cross-hairs of our rifles are on the back of your neck." The letter was constructed so that the last word came to a point on the bottom of the left side of the paper. I've never seen a letter before that was shaped like an arrow head. It must have taken a long time to compose a letter with that exact shape. I wondered what kind of person would take all the trouble to compose such a dramatic threat: it made me question whether I should continue my Saturday morning radio talk-show.

The unsigned letter made me reconsider my role as a radio talk-show host. At first, I disregarded the it, but my friends in law enforcement convinced me to take it seriously. Later I received an anonymous written message from a phone call at my office asking if I had received the "letter?" I decided the threat was real and I resigned my weekly radio show.

But I continued working with students who took my took political science courses. It was heartening to see what they did after graduation. Many went on to law school, some became campaign consultants or lobbyists, others became organizers for various unions, a few become college professors or teachers, one became a chamber of commerce executive, and another went on to become a member of the Oregon Supreme Court.

It is safe to assume that all of them came to see politics as a practical set of abilities developed by on-the-job experiences. One of the students proclaimed that "a degree in political science arms one with skills for life."

My students often made me feel proud.

THIRTY-ONE

A Matter of Perspective

O ne of my favorite syndicated columnists in the 1970s was Art Hoppe. He wrote about an assortment of intriguing things in life with a common-sense touch. Hoppe had an ability to turn the reader's head around to see something they overlooked before. I decided to invite him to speak on campus on the subject of how the nation was responding to the Vietnam War.

It was in the early 1970s when Art Hoppe came to Ashland from San Francisco. Protests against the Vietnam War were increasing across the country, college students were demonstrating on almost every campus, and US military causalities were climbing each week. The Nixon Administration was engaged in talks, but there wasn't much optimism about the future. I fully expected Hoppe would speak about the War.

I introduced Art Hoppe to the audience and he started out by saying he had just finished a "terribly sad week." He said his dog – who was his best friend – had been hit and killed by a car last Thursday night in front of his house. That same day, he said, eighty-seven American military personnel were killed in Vietnam. Hoppe said he cried himself to sleep that night. He hesitated for a long moment and added, "I cried for my dog."

Everyone in the audience, including me, was shocked. How could he compare the death of eighty-seven human beings to the death of a dog? He knew what we were thinking because he quickly denied that he was comparing the death of eighty-seven people to that of an animal, but he asked the audience to put themselves in his situation. How would they have responded?

He said it was really "a matter of perspective." He loved the dog. The dog was an emotional part of his life, but he didn't know any of the soldiers who were killed in Vietnam. Certainly, the military people who died where more important to the nation, but not to him – at least not last Thursday night. He said on that particular night, all he could think about was his dog. He blocked out everything else. Hoppe went on to say that everyone who has ever had a close pet that was unexpectedly killed would understand how that could become a pivotal day in his life. He repeated himself by saying, it was "a matter of perspective."

I always remembered that evening with Art Hoppe and how he explained his reaction to a traumatic event that affected his view of the world. Then I began to think that perhaps our whole nation might have had a similar reaction to upsetting or disastrous news – a time when their world changed forever – a time when they blocked out all other concerns.

It wasn't long before I started thinking about a very few events in recent times that really shocked this country and changed our perspective immediately. There have been just a few occurrences in modern history when the whole nation was overwhelmed by a single event. These were times when everyone could tell you where they were when they first heard the news. It was a moment when we knew that the world had changed, and our lives would never be the same again.

For my father's generation, everyone knew where they were

when they first learned about the Japanese attack on Pearl Harbor on December 7, 1941. I was nearly six years old at the time and I have only a vague memory, but I do recall that every adult in my life was worried after hearing the news. We were under an armed attack. It brought this country together like never before in history. Young men and women were compelled to enlist in the armed forces for the duration. No one knew how long it would last, but the American people were of one mind, they were dedicated to winning the war regardless of the cost. The commitment was shared by everyone regardless of age, race, gender or social class. When I was in grade school, we had a class project: to go out and convince our friends, neighbors and family to buy war bonds to defeat the enemy. Every day we kept track of our war bond sales on a chart with a picture of a B-17 bomber. Everyone realized it was a time of great personal sacrifice, but later Americans looked back at World War II as the "good war" because we were all working together in a common cause. Many years would go by before the country was brought together again in a state of shock.

Everyone in my generation can remember where they were on November 22, 1963 when they heard that President John F. Kennedy had been assassinated. I was in graduate school at the time, and I was meeting with a fellow student in a downtown hotel coffee shop. I looked up and noticed that the waitress, who was refilling our coffee cups, was crying uncontrollably. She poured coffee with one hand and wiped her eyes with the other. I asked if she was all right. She sobbed with a husky voice and said, "Don't you know the President is dead?" For the next four days everyone watched television in a sad silence as we felt the idealism of the John Kennedy era give way to a time of mourning and uncertainty. We had been led to believe that a new day was dawning with the inspiration of the Kennedy's New Frontier. His death made us feel like our generation had been robbed of a time to achieve great things. President Kennedy was not loved by everyone, but everyone was drawn together by his death. We were united not by affection for the dead President, but by our common sense of grieve that left us in a profound state of remorse.

The year 1968 was particularly difficult for the national psyche. There were several tragic events during that year when the whole country nearly went into a convulsion. Martin Luther King was shot to death on the fourth of April in Memphis. There was an immediate violent response as Black people and others realized that a great American leader had been slain because of his race. White and Black people alike felt a common loss in his death. The US Army was called in to stop the riots. Then on the fifth of June of that year, Robert Kennedy was gunned down in Los Angeles just as he was about to reclaim the Kennedy era and rekindle our aspirations. In his death, we realized how much Bobby meant to our hopes and dreams. For many of us, he was the future.

There were many who did not support either King or Kennedy, but they could feel that the nation had been dealt a serious blow. The year 1968 may have been the most divisive year in modern times. I recall thinking the nation was unraveling like a ball of yarn. It was different than any other time – we were coming apart at the seam. In a strange way, we were becoming united by our anger against each other. The word that described the rest of the century was that we were "polarized." There were deep divisions everywhere, but we were about to experience another historic event soon after that would bring us together in one day.

Everyone knows that September 11, 2001 was a clear day in New York City as two commercial airliners slammed into the

World Trade Center. That same day another hijacked plane hit the Pentagon while the fourth airliner was brought down by passengers before it could hit its expected target of either the US Capitol or the White House. Nearly 3,000 were killed and more than 6,000 were injured that day. The term "9/11" was coined and remembered by everyone. The American people were united in a way not seen since December 7, 1941. There were silent, impromptu candle vigils across the country. Firefighters and police officers from other states showed up in New York City to aid in the rescue and clearing of debris. I traveled back to Northern Ireland four days after 9/11. I went on BBC television in Belfast to explain the response of the American people. The Irish on both sides of the conflict had real tears for the United States. For a few days the conflict in Ulster was put aside. There were hundreds of flower bouquets placed in front of the US Consulate in Belfast. The French newspaper *La Monde* declared "We are all Americans." Queen Elisabeth II led the British nation singing, "God Bless America." President George W. Bush went to the crash site in New York City with the promise to track down those responsible for 9/11. The President's popularity topped out at nearly 90 percent.

December 7, 1941 and September 11, 2001 are often compared as being the only two occasions in modern times when the United States was invaded by an outside force. These two events generated a unity across the country that we had not known before or since. In both cases the response from American youth were similar – young people flocked to the recruiting office to enlist in the armed forces to fight the enemy. In both cases there was also an immediate preparation from the government to go after the enemy that had caused the invasion. But the comparisons end there.

In World War II we had an enemy that we could identify and

defeat, but the so-called war against terrorism that followed 9/11 had no legitimate target for our focus. It was a different world. The US invaded Iraq but the Iraqis were not even involved in the 9/11 attack. Then we spent twenty unsuccessful years fighting in Afghanistan. We were bogged down in an unwinnable war with dwindling public support. Somehow, we failed in our mission.

The national unity of World War II had left a positive memory for Americans as the "good war," but the unity of 2001 was squandered by fighting people who had little or nothing to do with 9/11. The American people sensed that they were being led in the wrong direction for the wrong reason.

Despite the confusion of 9/11, there was nothing to prepare us for the next time the nation would experience a sentinel moment when we knew that something was happening that would change our world forever. Beforehand, there was no expectation that January 6, 2021 would be a special day.

After being defeated for re-election in November of 2020, Donald Trump had invited his followers to come to Washington, D.C., for what he said would be a "wild" time. He had spent weeks formulating the "big lie" by which he claimed he had won the election, but that it had been "stolen" by fraudulent election practices. He never gave any details of the fraud, but he told his followers that they had to fight for their country or they would lose it. Several thousand followers showed up in Washington with flags, metal rods, bear spray, and clubs. They marched to the Capitol and stormed the building in an effort to stop the certification of the Electoral College vote.

The armed insurrection was well documented by video cameras installed in the Capitol building and also by cellphones belonging to the insurgents. The rioters overpowered the Capitol Police and went after Vice President Mike Pence and members of Congress who were in session certifying the 2020 election. It was a terribly upsetting day. Nothing even close to this had ever happened before in all of American history.

Like other fellow Americans, I watched the whole thing unfold on television. Along with others I had a feeling of disbelief as I watched the United States face an armed insurrection planned and implemented by other Americans. For the first time since the Civil War, we were turning on each other with the intent of overthrowing the government. It was not just a case of overzealous Americans protesting in front of the Capitol. We all saw the videos again and again. This was different than any of the marches and demonstrations we had ever seen in the past.

It was also different in that elected American officials were involved in encouraging the insurrection and those same leaders attempted to cover it up by trying to block a full investigation of the event. This was a one-of-a-kind happening that was aimed at undermining American democracy, and it was augmented by well-known elected officials who were in concert with thousands of people involved in an attempt to overthrow the dully elected government. Most of America could not believe what they were seeing on their television screens.

The insurrection of 2021 was dramatically different than the occurrences of 1941, 1963, 1968, and 2001. In those earlier years we shared the sense that we were in crisis together. Unity was our strength. American patriotism was at full bloom. We were driven together by a common desire to help each other. Events during those four years put the nation in a crisis mode, but our thoughts were centered on how we could pull together. All of that sounds corny until we remember how we really felt during those times when we thought of doing things that were good for the country, not just for ourselves or our political party. Our worst years brought out the best in us.

Earlier in these pages I noted a series of upsetting events that changed our national perspective in an instant because of a catastrophe that shook us as a people. But we recovered from those disasters because there was a path forward that could be taken. But now there are no visible guideposts. We've never been here before and we don't know what to do.

All the other stories in this book had an ending – a time when a particular experience could be analyzed with a lesson for the future. But this situation is different and much more serious. There's a raw quality about this conflict and it's not over.

Where are we going as a nation? No one knows.

About the Author

T he primary academic focus for Bill Meulemans has been the study of opposing political groups in the United States, Israel, and Northern Ireland. At the beginning of his career, he was appointed to a position at Southern Oregon College where he brought extremist group members of the left and right into his classroom. Meulemans developed models that illustrated the source of political attitudes and methods for resolving community conflicts. His primary focus was researching revolutionary groups of both the left and right. In addition, he spent time with the Hells Angels of Oakland, California, and other clandestine groups. At this point, his academic research was centered in Oregon and northern California, but later he moved into the southern and eastern United States to do interviews with members of the Ku Klux Klan and opposing racial groups in urban areas. He worked closely with professional organizations that developed techniques for resolving conflicts between minority groups and law enforcement agencies in Jersey City, New Jersey. Later, he expanded his research to include paramilitary groups in Israel and Northern Ireland. After a long tenure as a Professor of Political Science at Southern Oregon

University, Meulemans was awarded a Fulbright Scholarship to Israel. He spent his days with the Israelis in Jerusalem and his evenings with the Palestinians in Ramallah. One year later, he accepted a teaching post as Professor of Politics at The Queen's University of Belfast where he split his teaching duties with his research on paramilitary units in Northern Ireland. He conducted on-the-ground research while living in both Catholic and Protestant neighborhoods. After a decade in Ulster, he returned to the United States as a Professor of Political Science at Portland State University where he offered a course titled, "War and Peace in Northern Ireland."

In addition to his university work, Bill Meulemans was a staff aide in the US House of Representatives for the Committee on Education and Labor. He has written many articles and served on several boards and commissions in the United States and Northern Ireland. In a secondary role, he was a newspaper correspondent, a radio and television political commentator, and he also served as a political organizer for governmental agencies, business groups, ethic communities in conflict, and native people in western Oregon.

Bill Meulemans

www.hellgatepress.com